Docker

Unboxed

Mastering Modern Infrastructure with Container Technology

Sophia Bell

Table of Contents

Introduction

In the fast-paced and ever-evolving field of information technology, the idea of "containers" has emerged as a crucial and game-changing factor. Containerization ushers in a new era that is streamlined, productive, and scalable in contrast to the era of cumbersome virtual machines that are bloated and inefficient. Docker is the driving force behind this technological revolution. Docker has revolutionized the process through which software developers build, distribute, and run programs because of its capacity to enclose an application along with all of its dependencies into a single "container."

This is not just another technical manual; rather, "Docker Unboxed: Mastering Modern Infrastructure with Container Technology" provides a comprehensive guide to container technology. This e-book is an all-encompassing exploration into the enormous ocean that is Docker and container technologies. This e-book is designed for you if you are an IT professional who wants to modernize infrastructure, a developer who wants to increase productivity, or just a tech enthusiast who desires to understand the complexities of containerization.

Over the course of the chapters, we will dissect Docker from its most fundamental aspects all the way up to its most advanced and intricate ideas. In this e-book, we will talk about its architecture, its components, and its integration within the technology ecosystems of today. To ensure that you have a well-rounded educational experience, in addition to the theoretical expositions, you will also be given real-world case studies, hands-on activities, and recommendations for best practices.

Why should one use Docker? And why at this time? The demand for systems that are agile, scalable, and efficient is becoming more critical than it has ever been for businesses as they race toward digital transformation. Docker, with its promise of being able to "Build Once, Run Anywhere," provides a path toward reaching that future. It's not simply about picking up a new tool; rather, it's about adapting to a new way of thinking.

We have high hopes that by the time you have finished reading this e-book, not only will you have mastered the art and science of Docker, but you will also have an appreciation for its transformational potential. Docker allows you to dive in, discover, and take use of the power of modern infrastructure.

Chapter I

Docker Basics

Architecture: Images, Containers, Docker Daemon

The term "Docker," which has come to represent containerization in recent years, has been hailed as a game-changer that has altered the fundamental structure of software development and deployment. Underlying Docker's extensive ecosystem and community today is its core architecture, which consists of three components: Docker images, containers, and the Docker Daemon. In order to provide a thorough understanding of Docker's internal operations, this section delves deeply into the architecture of the program and explains the interactions and mechanisms among its three main parts.

The core attraction of Docker lies in its ability to provide consistency, portability, and isolation. Developers no longer complain the shortcomings of "it worked on my machine." Rather, Docker makes sure that an application that runs on a developer's workstation will also operate anywhere Docker is installed, whether that be on a production server in a remote data center, a testing environment, or a colleague's laptop. Most of the magic contained inside this promise is contained within Docker images and containers.

A blueprint is similar to a Docker image. It's a static snapshot with all the parts required to execute an application. The code, libraries, dependencies, and additional binaries of the application are included in this. A Docker image's immutability and mobility are what make it so appealing. An image doesn't change once it's formed. Because of its immutability, Docker images guarantee that you always operate with the same configuration, code, and dependencies, removing the variability that frequently results in software issues.

A Dockerfile contains a collection of instructions used to build Docker images. The base image to utilize (such a simple Linux distribution), the application code to copy into the image, any dependencies to install, and the configurations to apply are all described in this Dockerfile. A Docker image is produced when the Docker build command is run with this Dockerfile; it is then prepared for sharing, storing, or executing.

Docker registries make sharing and storing easier. The default public registry where developers may push their images and share them with the world is called Docker Hub, which is kept up to date by Docker Inc. Conversely, private registries enable businesses to maintain control and security over their images by storing them inside their infrastructure.

The Docker container is the house constructed using the blueprint, if the Docker image serves as the blueprint. A Docker image that is currently operating is called a container. It isolates the application from the host system and other containers, enclosing it in a secure environment. Namespaces allow for this isolation, guaranteeing that processes running inside a container are not aware of those running outside of it. Control groups, also known as cgroups, are another essential component of containers. They monitor and limit resource utilization, making that a containerized application only consumes the resources allotted to it.

Multiple containers can originate from a single Docker image. Every container has its own filesystem that is derived from the image it is instantiated from and works in its own isolated environment. Any modifications made to a container's filesystem are lost upon deletion. Nonetheless, Docker offers tools for setting up persistent storage, guaranteeing that information is kept safe even in the event that the container is shut down.

Docker Daemon is the one that controls the complex movement between images and containers. Docker container management is done by this background process, which also interacts with Docker images, containers, networks, and storage in addition to responding to commands from the Docker CLI (Command-Line Interface). Building images from Dockerfiles, launching containers from these images, guaranteeing container security and isolation, and interacting with Docker registries to push or pull images are all handled by the Docker Daemon.

Other programs or even distant clients can communicate with the Docker Daemon over its REST API. Because of this architecture, developers can use the Docker CLI or any other tool that can interface with the Docker API to interact with the Docker Daemon remotely, even if it is operating on a server in a data center. Because an organization can have a centralized Docker Daemon monitoring containers while developers and operators interface with it from their devices, the decoupling of the Daemon and the CLI ensures flexibility and scalability.

A few guiding principles support the synergistic interaction that exists between Docker images, containers, and the Docker Daemon. Efficiency is the first: Docker containers are lightweight and quick because, in contrast to virtual machines, they share the host system's kernel instead of simulating a whole operating system. Another is portability; because Docker images are self-contained and consistent, they guarantee that programs operate consistently no matter where they are installed. Lastly, simplicity - Docker ensures that developers can concentrate on creating code rather than maintaining infrastructure by providing a straightforward user interface to its users, even with its intricate internal workings.

In conclusion, Docker's strong architecture is responsible for its revolutionary influence on the software industry. Docker created a paradigm that guarantees consistency, isolation, and efficiency by conceiving the distinction between images (the blueprint) and containers (the real application). Unnoticed yet indispensable, the Docker Daemon quietly handles the intricacies so developers can work with ease. Docker's concept and promise are embodied by the trinity of Docker images, containers, and the Docker Daemon, which makes it an essential tool for contemporary software development and deployment.

Installing Docker

A constant state of innovation has characterized the progress of software development and deployment, with each new breakthrough seeking to streamline and improve the associated processes. Docker has emerged as a revolutionary tool in this never-ending quest for efficiency, making containerization accessible to a wider audience. For developers, DevOps specialists, and system administrators, Docker has become an essential tool because it guarantees consistency, isolation, and portability. However, Docker needs to be installed correctly before it can be used to its full potential. This section goes further into the Docker installation process, emphasizing the subtleties that vary between operating systems, the things to remember, and the post-installation procedures that guarantee a positive Docker experience.

The first step in the installation process is to comprehend the requirements. Docker is a platform that creates and manages containers via OS-level virtualization. This indicates that the host operating system is very important. Docker can run on the majority of 64-bit current machines, though the specifics vary depending on the operating system.

Since Linux is where containers first appeared, it provides a native and seamless Docker experience. Within the default repositories of the majority of popular distributions, such as Fedora, Ubuntu, Debian, and CentOS, there are Docker packages available. However, installing Docker from the official Docker repositories is frequently advised to guarantee that you're getting the most recent version.

Typically, the procedure entails installing Docker, updating the package database, and configuring the Docker repository.

Although the instructions may vary slightly between distributions, the general idea stays the same. For example, to update the system, add the Docker repository, and install Docker on an Ubuntu machine, use the apt commands. Docker operates as a daemon after installation, therefore it's usually advantageous to allow it to launch upon boot. Another benefit of Linux is that it provides a smooth Docker CLI experience, enabling users to work with Docker directly from the terminal.

Windows was not Docker's natural home at first, despite its large user base. Docker has gained traction, nevertheless, after the release of Hyper-V and Windows Subsystem for Linux (WSL). For Windows, the suggested installation method is Docker Desktop. This program offers a graphical user interface (or GUI) and smoothly incorporates Docker into Windows.

Hyper-V must be enabled before installing Docker Desktop, since Docker leverages it for virtualization. Assuming the necessary conditions are satisfied, installing Docker requires just downloading the Docker Desktop application from the official Docker website and following the prompts on the screen. Once installed, users can use PowerShell or the Windows command prompt to interface with Docker using the Docker CLI, much like on Linux.

Mac users can also benefit from the Docker adventure. Users of macOS can enjoy a seamless installation process with Docker

Desktop for Mac. Docker Desktop uses the macOS Hypervisor.framework for virtualization internally. The Docker Desktop application must be downloaded from the Docker website and then dropped into the Applications folder in order to be installed.

Verifying the installation is essential after installation on any operating system. To verify the Docker version installed, run a command such as docker --version. Additionally, the well-known "docker run hello-world" acts as a rite of passage, guaranteeing that Docker is installed correctly and capable of pulling images and launching containers.

Users can apply various setups and considerations after installation. Docker can be set up to launch automatically at boot, guaranteeing that the daemon is constantly up and ready. Docker provides proxy configurations for people using proxies in order to guarantee seamless network operations. In accordance with user needs, storage and network configurations can also be changed.

It's also critical to comprehend the security implications of Docker. Docker needs root access by default, which raises security issues. To reduce these concerns, Docker offers features like user namespaces. Users should think about creating Docker registries after installation so they can push and pull Docker images. Although the official public registry is Docker Hub, companies frequently create private registries of their own to store their images.

In conclusion, even if installing Docker is simple, it still necessitates knowledge of the underlying operating system and its nuances.

Docker guarantees a consistent experience whether you're using Windows, utilizing Hyper-V and WSL, or adopting the native habitat of containers on Linux, macOS, or Windows. But installation is only the first step. The actual process is creating Docker images, launching containers, managing them, and ultimately launching high-performing, scalable applications. The simplicity of the first configuration conceals Docker's tremendous potential, which are just waiting to be unlocked by those willing to go deeper—as with any powerful tool.

Basic Docker commands

In the vast landscape of modern software infrastructure, Docker stands as a beacon of innovation and efficiency. At its core, Docker's power and flexibility come from its command-line interface, which provides users with a rich set of tools to interact with, manage, and orchestrate containers. For both neophytes and veterans of Docker, mastering these commands is essential. These basic commands are the foundation upon which the intricate edifice of containerized applications is built.

A user will likely encounter the docker run command when first embarking on the Docker journey. This command might seem simple at a glance, but it embodies the essence of Docker's purpose. With docker run, you can initiate a container from a specified image, bringing an application to life. This command seamlessly combines several steps – pulling an image if it's unavailable locally, creating a container from that image, and starting it. Such condensed power represents Docker's philosophy: reducing the complexity of operations while maintaining efficacy.

However, before running containers, one often interacts with Docker images, and for this, the docker pull and docker push commands are indispensable. The docker pull command fetches an image from Docker Hub or any other configured registry. It ensures that developers and operators can access standardized application environments, irrespective of their location. Conversely, docker push allows users to upload their custom images to registries, making them accessible to teams and tools across the globe. By mastering these commands, one ensures the fluidity of Docker images, moving them across systems and environments.

But, as containers multiply and applications scale, managing them becomes paramount. The docker ps command becomes a staple in this context. It gives users a snapshot of all running containers, offering insights into their IDs, names, status, and ports. For a broader perspective, appending the -a option reveals all containers, regardless of their status, granting operators a holistic view of their environment.

Amidst managing these containers, the need often arises to delve into the internals of a running container. The docker exec command is the gateway to such interactivity. With it, users can run specified commands inside a container. Whether it's brief shell access via docker exec -it container_name /bin/sh or executing specific application diagnostics, this command ensures operators can seamlessly intervene and interact with their containerized applications.

As containers are temporary by nature, understanding their lifecycle becomes vital. The trio of docker start, stop, and restart commands are central to this. With these commands at one's fingertips, containers can be gracefully started, halted, or rebooted. Such control ensures that operators can precisely manage application uptime, maintenance windows, and updates.

Yet, as applications evolve, so do their environments. Occasionally, one might need to inspect the configuration and filesystem of a Docker object closely. With its detailed JSON output, the docker inspect command provides an in-depth perspective on containers and images. Whether it's to fetch IP addresses, volume paths, or intricate settings, this command acts as a magnifying glass, revealing the minutiae of Docker objects.

Furthermore, in the course of operations, it's not uncommon to amass a collection of unused containers, dangling images, or orphaned volumes. The docker system prune command emerges as a housekeeping hero in such scenarios. A single invocation clears out unused Docker objects, ensuring system hygiene and optimized resource utilization.

Finally, mastering Docker commands would be incomplete without acknowledging the docker build command. For those crafting custom Docker images, this command stands as a cornerstone. Docker build constructs a Docker image layer by layer by interpreting the instructions in a Dockerfile. This iterative process ensures that applications and their dependencies are cohesively bundled, and ready for deployment.

In the grand tapestry of Docker, these commands represent just the foundational threads. Yet, their mastery is crucial. They encapsulate the most common tasks and challenges faced when working with Docker. As one deepens their understanding and practice with these commands, the broader horizons of Docker – from orchestration with Docker Compose to advanced networking and storage configurations – become accessible and intuitive.

In conclusion, Docker's command-line interface is more than just a set of commands; it's a language of containerization. By fluently speaking this language, developers and operators bridge the gap between code and deployment, ensuring that applications are built with excellence and delivered with the efficiency, scalability, and resilience that modern infrastructures demand.

Chapter II

Understanding Docker Images

What is a Docker Image?

In the annals of software development and deployment, Docker is an emblem of transformative innovation. Its influence extends from individual developers' workstations to global-scale production environments. At the heart of Docker's success and its promise of consistent, scalable, and isolated application deployment lies a fundamental concept: the Docker Image. This singular construct has reshaped our approach to software lifecycle management, and understanding its essence is pivotal for anyone delving into the world of containerization.

At a high level, a Docker Image can be conceptualized as a snapshot or a static representation of an application and its entire environment. This encapsulation includes the application code, runtime, system libraries, tools, and other files needed for its execution. This all-encompassing nature of Docker Images ensures applications run identically, irrespective of where the Docker container is instantiated.

Peeling back the layers of a Docker Image reveals a sophisticated structure that maximizes efficiency and minimizes redundancy. Images are composed of multiple layers, each representing a distinct filesystem change. These layers are stacked upon one another, with each subsequent layer only capturing the difference from the previous one. Such an approach offers dual advantages. Firstly, it promotes reusability. Common layers shared across multiple images must be downloaded or stored only once, significantly saving bandwidth and storage. Secondly, it ensures immutability. Once a layer is created, it cannot be altered. This fixed nature guarantees that the application environment remains consistent across deployments, eliminating the notorious "it works on my machine" syndrome.

This layered architecture of Docker Images owes its elegance to the union filesystem. By overlaying multiple read-only layers with a writable layer on top, Docker can construct a single cohesive filesystem. This means that while the underlying layers remain unchanged, any modification, whether a new file addition or an existing file change, is reflected in the topmost writable layer. This delicate balance between read-only and writable layers guarantees data persistence during the container's lifecycle while maintaining the foundational immutability of the Docker Image.

Creating a Docker Image is a meticulously choreographed dance of instructions, typically articulated in a Dockerfile. This plain-text file serves as a blueprint, guiding Docker through the steps required to craft the desired environment. It might prescribe tasks like setting a base image, installing necessary software, copying application code, or defining environmental variables. The docker build command then interprets this Dockerfile, executing each instruction in sequence. The result is a new image layer for every instruction, gradually building up the final Docker Image, ready to be instantiated as a container.

While developers have the liberty to create custom images tailored to their applications, the beauty of Docker lies in its vast communal ecosystem. Repositories like Docker Hub serve as public libraries, hosting many pre-built images for various software, tools, and applications. Whether it's a vanilla operating system, a database server, or a sophisticated machine learning framework, chances are there's already a Docker Image available. This communal sharing accelerates deployment and ensures that users can leverage best practices and optimizations from the broader community.

Moreover, the Docker Image's role isn't just confined to local development or individual deployments. In modern CI/CD pipelines, Docker Images have emerged as the currency of software delivery. Once an image encapsulating an application version is created, it can be pushed to image repositories. From there, it can be pulled and deployed across various stages of the software delivery lifecycle, from integration testing environments to staging and finally to production. Such a flow ensures that the exact environment vetted during testing is what gets deployed in production, eliminating discrepancies and promoting reliability.

In conclusion, the Docker Image is a cornerstone in container technology's edifice. It encapsulates the brilliance of Docker's philosophy—providing a consistent, isolated, and efficient environment for applications. By packaging an application and its world within an image, Docker has nullified the challenges posed by varying deployment environments, setting a new gold standard for software delivery. With its layered architecture, immutability, and communal ecosystem, the Docker Image is more than just a technical construct. It is a testament to Docker's vision of a world where software can be developed, shipped, and run with unparalleled ease and confidence, irrespective of its complexity or scale. For developers and operators, understanding the nuances of Docker Images is not just beneficial—it's essential in navigating the evolving terrain of modern software infrastructure.

Creating your first Docker Image

Embarking on the Docker journey heralds a paradigm shift for many developers and infrastructure specialists. While Docker's overarching benefits in consistency, scalability, and isolation are widely celebrated, the process often begins with a single, foundational step: creating your very first Docker image. This endeavor, emblematic of Docker's philosophy of simplicity and efficiency, opens doors to the vast world of containerized deployments. As we delve into the nuances of this initiation, it's imperative to understand the guiding principles and practices that underlie this transformative technology.

At its core, every Docker image begins its life as a plain-text script known as the Dockerfile. This document is the soul of your Docker image, a step-by-step guide that Docker follows, ensuring every requisite component of your application environment is meticulously accounted for. It's in the Dockerfile that a developer's intentions for the environment, the application's needs, and Docker's capabilities converge.

Starting with the Dockerfile, a pivotal decision awaits: selecting a base image. Docker images are inherently hierarchical. Rather than starting from scratch, most Dockerfiles build upon existing images, layering on a specific application's unique components and configurations. These base images, often sourced from Docker Hub, range from minimalist Linux distributions like Alpine to specialized environments tailored for languages like Python or Node.js. The choice of a base image lays the groundwork for what follows, ensuring that foundational software, libraries, and configurations are already in place.

Once the base is set, the real customization begins. Through a series of Dockerfile instructions, one molds the image to the application's precise needs. The RUN instruction is a primary tool in this process, allowing the execution of shell commands. Whether updating package lists, installing software, or tweaking configurations, RUN facilitates these tasks, ensuring the image mirrors the desired state.

However, an image isn't just about the environment; it's equally about the application it serves. Here, the COPY and ADD instructions come to the fore. While both are geared toward transferring files from the host system into the image, COPY is straightforward and recommended for most use cases, whereas ADD possesses additional capabilities, like handling remote URLs and auto-extracting archives. With these instructions, application source code, assets, scripts, and configuration files find their way into the Docker image.

Yet, an environment and application alone don't define an image's behavior. The Dockerfile's CMD and ENTRYPOINT instructions impart the image with a sense of purpose. They determine what command or process launches when a container is instantiated from the image. Whether starting a web server, initializing a database, or running an application script, these instructions breathe life into the image, turning it from a static environment into a dynamic entity ready to perform.

Fine-tuning often accompanies this crafting process. One can set environment variables through ENV instructions, providing configurable parameters for the application. With WORKDIR, a working directory inside the container can be defined, ensuring that subsequent commands operate in the desired location. On the other hand, the EXPOSE instruction signals that the containerized application will listen on specific network ports, preparing the stage for network interactions once the container is up and running.

With the Dockerfile crafted, the next phase is the actual image creation. This is accomplished through the docker build command. When executed, Docker reads the Dockerfile, executing each instruction in sequence. Docker captures the resulting state as a new image layer as each step completes. This layering, as previously discussed, ensures efficiency and promotes reusability.

After the build process, a Docker image emerges, a cohesive environment ready to house your application. With tools like docker images, you can marvel at your creation, view its details, and understand its size. And the true magic unfolds when you employ the docker run command, bringing your first Docker image to life as a running container.

In conclusion, creating a Docker image blends art and science. It's where a developer's understanding of their application melds with Docker's capabilities to produce a consistent, scalable, and isolated environment. Crafting your first Docker image is more than a technical exercise; it's an initiation into a world of possibilities, where the boundaries between development, testing, and deployment blur, giving rise to a streamlined, efficient, and agile software lifecycle. And as with any craft, mastery comes with practice. As you refine, rebuild, and reimagine your Docker images, you're not just creating containers but shaping the future of software infrastructure.

Managing and distributing Docker Images

In the theater of software development, Docker has positioned itself as both the maestro and the magician, orchestrating applications in isolated environments and conjuring consistent deployments across disparate systems. But once the feat of creating a Docker image is accomplished, a new set of challenges arises—how does one effectively manage these images and ensure they're accessible to collaborators or deployment systems wherever needed? The narrative of Docker's prowess is incomplete without understanding the mechanisms that facilitate the storage, retrieval, and distribution of Docker images.

Central to the Docker image management paradigm is the container registry concept—a specialized repository designed to store and distribute Docker images. This registry, similar to version control systems for code, is a single source of truth, ensuring that once an image is committed, it remains unaltered and can be reliably retrieved for future deployments. Docker's own public registry, Docker Hub, is perhaps the most well-known in this arena. Offering a vast library of both official and community-contributed images, Docker Hub has emerged as the default rendezvous point for developers seeking pre-configured environments or base images to scaffold their Dockerfile designs.

However, Docker Hub isn't alone in this landscape. The growing ubiquity of containerized deployments has ushered in a proliferation of alternative container registries. Cloud providers, recognizing the centrality of Docker in modern infrastructure, have rolled out their offerings—Google Container Registry, Amazon Elastic Container Registry, and Azure Container Registry, to name a few. While fulfilling the fundamental role of a container registry, these services often come integrated with additional features tailored for cloud-native deployments, such as enhanced security scanning, fine-grained access controls, and integrations with other cloud services.

Private container registries surface as the solution for organizations or individuals wary of entrusting their Docker images to public registries—either due to proprietary nature, security concerns, or compliance mandates. By hosting a private registry, whether on-premise or in a chosen cloud environment, users can ensure that their Docker images remain accessible only to authorized entities. Docker's own solution, Docker Trusted Registry, exemplifies this model, offering an enterprise-grade, self-hosted variant of Docker Hub with augmented security and management features.

Whether public or private, once an image is crafted and tested, it must be committed to a registry. This process, often called 'pushing,' is initiated with the docker push command. Before an image can be pushed, however, it must be appropriately tagged with the registry's address, ensuring Docker knows the destination. Once pushed, the image, now residing in the registry, can be 'pulled' by anyone with appropriate permissions, using the docker pull command. This push-pull dynamic ensures that whether you're a developer sharing your image with a global audience, a team collaborating on a project, or an automated deployment system provisioning infrastructure, the desired Docker image is just a command away.

Yet, managing Docker images is about more than just storage and retrieval. Effective organization becomes paramount with the multitude of images, versions, and variants that can accumulate. This is where image tagging shines. Custom tags can be employed beyond the latest tag, which represents the most recent version of an image. Whether denoting specific versions, feature branches, or environment configurations, these tags ensure that the correct image variant is employed for the right task.

An essential, often under-discussed, facet of Docker image distribution is security. Given that a Docker image encapsulates the entire runtime environment of an application, vulnerabilities within an image can have far-reaching implications. Recognizing this, Docker and third-party registry providers often embed security scanning features. These tools automatically scrutinize pushed images, identifying known vulnerabilities in the software and libraries contained therein. By integrating these scans into CI/CD pipelines, developers can be alerted to potential security threats before an image reaches a production environment.

In conclusion, while creating a Docker image is undeniably a milestone in the containerization journey, the subsequent management and distribution of these images are where the collaborative magic happens. By leveraging container registries, be it public offerings like Docker Hub or private, self-hosted solutions, developers and organizations can ensure their images are stored, organized, and accessible, underpinning the promise of consistent deployments. Add to this the safety net of security scanning, and Docker image management becomes a harmonious blend of accessibility, organization, and security. In a world rapidly embracing containerized deployments, understanding these intricacies isn't just advantageous—it's essential for any software professional aiming to harness the full power of Docker.

Chapter III

Docker Containers

Lifecyle of a Docker Container

In the sprawling tapestry of modern software infrastructure, Docker containers have become emblematic of ephemeral computing—instances born from a specification, executing their duties, and vanishing back into the void. But beneath this transience lies a structured lifecycle, a sequence of states and transitions that govern the existence of every Docker container. By delving into this lifecycle, we glean insights into the principles underpinning Docker's agility and efficiency, laying bare the mechanics of container orchestration in intricate detail.

At the heart of every Docker container's lifecycle lies its progenitor: the Docker image. Think of this image as a blueprint—a static, immutable specification encapsulating everything the container will need, from the operating system and libraries to the application and its dependencies. The chosen Docker image sets the stage before a container takes its first breath, ensuring a consistent and reproducible environment.

A container's life begins in earnest with the docker create command. This act of creation instantiates a new container from the specified image, but the container remains dormant, a mere potentiality awaiting activation. It's worth noting that while often overlooked in favor of more holistic commands, this creation step is foundational, setting parameters like network configurations, storage volumes, and environment variables that will influence the container's subsequent behavior.

The docker start command triggers the transition from dormancy to activity. With this, the container springs to life, initializing its environment and executing the default command or the entrypoint specified in its Docker image. This active state, often termed 'running,' is where the container fulfills its purpose, be it serving a web application, processing data, or running a database. In this phase, the container behaves like any other running process on the host system, albeit encapsulated within its isolated environment.

However, the beauty of Docker lies not just in starting containers but in managing them throughout their lifecycle. While a container runs, developers and administrators can interact with it using various commands. The docker logs command, for instance, provides a window into the container's soul, displaying output logs that offer insights into its behavior. Simultaneously, the docker exec command allows one to step into the container's environment, executing commands within its isolated context, a valuable tool for debugging or configuration.

Yet, the lifecycle of a Docker container is as much about cessation as it is about activity. When a container's task is complete, or if it needs to be temporarily halted, the docker stop command comes into play. This command gracefully terminates the container, allowing any running processes to conclude before the container transitions to a 'stopped' state. But termination needn't be the end. A stopped container can be resurrected, returning to active duty with another docker start command. This cyclical nature of starting and stopping underlines the flexibility of Docker containers, allowing them to be reused, reducing the overhead of constant creation and destruction.

However, there are moments when a container has served its purpose entirely or needs to be removed due to system constraints. In these scenarios, the docker rm command facilitates the container's final farewell, removing it from the system and freeing associated resources. This removal underscores the ephemerality inherent to Docker containers—entities designed for transient tasks, leaving little trace once their duty is done.

Yet, even in cessation, the lessons and insights garnered from a container's life remain invaluable. Docker provides mechanisms like the docker diff command to discern changes made to a container's filesystem, offering clues about its behavior and interactions. Furthermore, the state and configuration of a running or stopped container can be immortalized in a new Docker image utilizing the docker commit command. This capability, reminiscent of snapshots, allows developers to capture a container's essence, providing a foundation for future containers or serving as a record of unique configurations and states.

In conclusion, while seemingly simple, the lifecycle of a Docker container is a dance of creation, activity, cessation, and removal. Each phase, governed by specific commands and transitions, offers unique opportunities for interaction, management, and insight. This structured lifecycle underpins Docker's promise of consistency and agility, ensuring that containers can be rapidly instantiated, managed, and removed in alignment with the ever-changing needs of modern software deployments. By understanding this lifecycle, we not only demystify the operations of Docker containers but also equip ourselves to harness their full potential, optimizing processes, conserving resources, and ensuring seamless software delivery in the age of containerization.

Starting, Stopping, and Managing Containers

As the software world embraces containerization, Docker, with its promise of encapsulated, consistent, and lightweight deployments, has become the conductor of an intricate ballet. This ballet involves orchestrating containers—ephemeral entities designed for singular tasks—through various stages of their existence. Starting, stopping, and managing these containers may seem like rudimentary actions on the surface, but by delving deeper, we uncover a realm of granularity, precision, and flexibility, reflecting the true spirit of modern software operations.

Though temporary by nature, Docker containers require a structured approach to their lifecycle to maintain efficiency and order. This approach is primarily governed by commands that allow users to manipulate the state and behavior of containers. One of the first user interactions with a container is initiating its life using the docker run command. This command is more than just a starter; it's a conjurer, bringing to life a container from an image while simultaneously allowing users to specify parameters like networking options, mount points, and environment variables. The beauty of docker run lies in its dual nature: it creates and then immediately starts the container, setting the stage for the tasks it is designed to perform.

However, while the act of creation and starting is crucial, the ability to introspect and manage a running container is equally vital. Once active, a container might require real-time interaction, especially if it's serving a pivotal role in an application stack. The docker exec command serves this purpose, allowing users to execute commands inside the running container for debugging, data retrieval, or configuration tweaks. Additionally, the docker logs command acts as a bridge, relaying messages and outputs from the container to the user, aiding in monitoring and troubleshooting.

Yet, in the ever-shifting landscape of software operations, not all containers are meant to run indefinitely. Some might complete their tasks swiftly, while others need to be paused for resource conservation or maintenance. The command docker stop is the gentle whisper that signals a container to cease its operations. Elegant in its operation, it provides a grace period for the container to conclude any running processes before halting. But the dance isn't over; stopped containers can be awakened using the docker start command, a testament to Docker's flexibility.

The choreography extends beyond mere starting and stopping. Sometimes, the need arises to momentarily freeze a container without entirely stopping it, especially when diagnosing performance issues or managing resource consumption. The docker pause command introduces this temporary stasis, suspending the container's processes. When the moment of introspection or conservation passes, the container can resume its rhythm with the docker unpause command.

In scenarios where containers serve temporary or experimental purposes, they might accumulate, occupying valuable system resources. The management of these dormant containers becomes pivotal. With the docker rm command, users can remove individual or multiple containers, ensuring that the system remains clutter-free. Moreover, to oversee the myriad containers that might exist in various states, the docker ps command acts as the sentinel, listing containers, their statuses, and essential metadata, providing a panoramic view of the container landscape.

As containers meander through their lifecycle, they might change—configurations might be tweaked, software might be updated, or data might be generated. Capturing these changes can offer valuable insights or serve as a foundation for future deployments. Docker introduces the concept of container checkpoints, allowing users to save the current state of a container, which can later be restored or even migrated to another system. This mechanism, leveraging the docker checkpoint commands, adds another layer of flexibility, ensuring that no valuable state is lost in the dynamic world of container operations.

In conclusion, while lightweight and transient, Docker containers carry the weight of modern software operations on their shoulders. To ensure they dance to the right tunes, Docker offers a suite of commands that facilitate creation, management, introspection, and cessation. These commands, far from mere operational tools, embody the principles of agility, flexibility, and efficiency, hallmarks of containerized deployments. By mastering the ballet of starting, stopping, and managing containers, users optimize their Docker experience and pave the way for seamless, consistent, and scalable software deployments, resonating with the ethos of contemporary software delivery.

Docker Container Networking and Storage

Docker has crystallized its reputation in software development and deployment as a beacon of containerization, heralding an era where encapsulation, consistency, and agility are paramount. While the fundamental appeal of Docker lies in its promise to package software in discrete units, the success of these containers heavily rests on their ability to interact with the outside world and retain data—two tasks executed with finesse through Docker's networking and storage capabilities. While technical, these two facets are the arteries and veins of the Docker ecosystem, ensuring that containers are not isolated islands but integrated components in the vast landscape of software infrastructure.

Let's embark first on the journey of networking within Docker. At its core, Docker adopts a philosophy of isolation. Each container is bestowed with its network namespace, ensuring it operates within its enclave. But to facilitate communication between containers or external networks, Docker employs many networking drivers. The default driver, aptly named the 'bridge driver,' creates a private internal network on the host system, assigning IP addresses to each container. This ensures that containers can communicate seamlessly while remaining insulated from the host.

However, Docker's networking prowess doesn't stop here. Recognizing the varied networking demands of applications, Docker offers the 'host driver,' allowing a container to share the host's network namespace, and the 'overlay driver,' perfect for facilitating communication between containers sprawled across multiple host systems in a swarm. For those scenarios demanding complete network isolation, the 'none driver' ensures containers operate in their secluded network namespace, detached from external communications. Yet, beyond these drivers, Docker also allows users to define custom networks, catering to bespoke application requirements and ensuring optimal communication pathways.

Parallel to the avenues of networking, the alleyways of Docker storage are equally intricate and pivotal. After all, in the dynamic world of containers, where instances are created, destroyed, and recreated in rapid succession, data persistence becomes a holy grail. Docker containers, in their native state, possess a temporary filesystem. Any data generated or modified within a container risks oblivion once the container is terminated. To combat this transience and ensure data longevity, Docker introduces the concept of volumes.

Docker volumes, detached from the fleeting life cycle of containers, offer a persistent storage mechanism. These are directories—residing outside the container's filesystem—but mountable within containers, allowing data to be read or written. The sheer beauty of volumes lies in their reusability; a volume can be detached from one container and attached to another, ensuring that data remains accessible and consistent across container lifecycles. Moreover, Docker volumes are managed by Docker itself, abstracting away the underlying storage complexities and offering a seamless interface for data operations.

But Docker's storage narrative is further enriched by bind and tmpfs mounts. Bind mounts, like volumes, allow data to be shared between the container and the host system. However, they are inherently tied to the host's filesystem, granting containers access to specific directories or files on the host. This mechanism is beneficial for scenarios demanding real-time data synchronization between the host and containers. Tmpfs mounts, on the other hand, introduce a layer of volatility, creating a temporary filesystem in the host's memory, accessible to the container. While unsuitable for persistent data, this temporary storage offers fast read and write operations, perfect for temporary data processing tasks.

In conclusion, Docker's networking and storage capabilities, while often overshadowed by the allure of containerization, are the lifeblood of the Docker ecosystem. While isolated in their operations, they ensure that containers remain communicative, integrated, and data-consistent entities in the software landscape. By providing many networking drivers and flexible storage mechanisms, Docker addresses the multifaceted demands of modern applications and reinforces its commitment to agility, efficiency, and consistency. Thus, as we weave through the labyrinth of Docker, it becomes evident that its strength lies not just in encapsulating software but in connecting and preserving it, echoing the holistic vision of integrated and resilient software infrastructure.

Chapter IV

Docker Compose

Introduction to Orchestration with Docker Compose

Amidst the vast universe of software deployment, Docker emerged as a stellar entity, transforming how we perceive and manage applications. Its containers brought forth an unparalleled promise: to encapsulate applications and their dependencies in isolated, consistent, and replicable units. Yet, as applications grew in complexity, spanning multiple containers, there arose a need for an orchestrator, a maestro to harmonize this symphony of containers. Introducing Docker Compose, Docker's in-house conductor, designed to facilitate creating and managing multi-container Docker applications.

To truly appreciate the significance of Docker Compose, one must first recognize the challenges it addresses. Contemporary applications seldom operate in isolation. They are often a confluence of multiple services—a database, a backend API, a front-end server, perhaps a caching layer, and more. Each of these services can be encapsulated within a Docker container. However, manually deploying and managing these intertwined containers is labor-intensive and prone to errors. The intricate web of inter-container communications, shared volumes, and coordinated starts and stops can quickly transform into an operational nightmare. With its declarative approach to defining and running multi-container applications, Docker Compose emerges as the beacon of simplicity and efficiency amidst this potential chaos.

At the heart of Docker Compose is the docker-compose.yml file—a declarative YAML file that allows developers to define all the services, networks, and volumes an application needs. Instead of juggling a plethora of docker run commands, users can describe the entire application stack in this singular file. Each service represents a container, and the configuration options mirror the flags and parameters one would use with the Docker CLI. Be it setting environment variables, mounting volumes, defining network connections, or scaling instances, everything is articulable within this configuration file.

Docker Compose's ability to recognize the interdependencies between services makes it exceptionally powerful. By using the depends_on field, developers can specify the order in which services are started, ensuring that, for instance, a web service only begins once the database it relies on is fully operational. Furthermore, Docker Compose automatically sets up a dedicated network for all the services defined, ensuring they can communicate with each other seamlessly while remaining isolated from external networks. This dedicated networking, combined with service names as DNS entries, ensures that inter-service communications are both possible and intuitive.

But the magic of Docker Compose isn't just confined to its declarative nature. With a suite of commands, Docker Compose makes managing the application's lifecycle remarkably easy. The docker-compose up command reads the docker-compose.yml file and brings the entire application stack to life, starting services according to their dependencies and ensuring they operate harmoniously. Conversely, docker-compose down halts this symphony, gracefully stopping all services and cleaning up networks and volumes. And for those who crave introspection, commands like docker-compose logs or docker-compose ps offer insights into the running services, their records, and their statuses.

However, as much as Docker Compose excels in local development and testing environments, one must understand its limitations. It is primarily tailored for single-host deployments. For multi-host scenarios or when high availability and failover strategies are paramount, orchestration tools like Kubernetes or Docker Swarm might be more suitable. Yet, Docker Compose can act as a stepping stone, familiarizing users with multi-container orchestration principles and preparing them for more complex orchestrators.

In the grand concert of software deployment, while Docker introduced the pristine notes of containerization, Docker Compose emerged as the maestro, harmonizing these notes into a coherent and harmonious symphony. By abstracting the complexities of multi-container deployments into a singular, declarative configuration file and offering an intuitive command suite, Docker Compose not only simplified the orchestration process but also democratized it, making multi-container applications accessible to both novices and experts alike. In doing so, it didn't just amplify Docker's promise but also showcased the future of software deployment—a future where applications, irrespective of their complexity, can be defined, deployed, and managed with elegance and ease.

Writing a docker-compose.yml file

The narrative of Docker's rise in the technological ecosystem is akin to a riveting novel, with each chapter unveiling innovations that revolutionized software deployment. While Docker containers laid the foundational framework, the docker-compose.yml file emerged as the blueprint, guiding the orchestrated dance of multi-container applications. Through the seemingly plain text of this YAML file, developers could conjure intricate software infrastructures, defining not just the containers, but the ligaments that bind them—the networks, volumes, and dependencies. Let's immerse ourselves in the art of crafting this pivotal document, exploring the nuances and intricacies that breathe life into complex applications.

Envision the docker-compose.yml file as an architect's plan. Just as a house is composed of rooms serving different purposes, interconnected by doors and hallways, an application often comprises several services (containers), linked by networks and sharing data through volumes. The primary responsibility of the docker-compose.yml file is to provide a comprehensive, yet concise, description of this multifaceted structure.

The file often begins by declaring the version of Docker Compose being used. This version dictates the features and syntax available, ensuring that the Compose file remains consistent across varying environments. Following the version declaration, the heart of the file is segmented into primary sections: services, networks, and volumes.

In the realm of the docker-compose.yml file, the services section is undoubtedly the epicenter. It's here that each container is described, echoing its unique role in the application's universe. Each service corresponds to a Docker image, which can be a pre-built image from a repository like Docker Hub or one crafted using a local Dockerfile. The attributes under each service serve to fine-tune its behavior. For instance, the environment attribute allows one to set environment variables within the container, and the ports attribute maps container ports to the host machine, thereby governing external access. Moreover, it's within this section that inter-service dependencies are articulated. Using the depends_on attribute, one can dictate the order of service startup, ensuring, for example, that a web server only ignites after its underlying database has fully awakened.

But an application's architecture isn't merely about isolated services; it's equally about the channels of communication that bind them. The networks section of the docker-compose.yml file carves out these channels, defining custom networks that facilitate inter-container communication. Docker Compose automatically sets up a default network for the defined services, but custom networks become indispensable for scenarios demanding segmented communication pathways or specific network configurations. By associating services with these networks, developers can finetune the communicative interactions of their application components.

While services and networks define an application's active components and pathways, the volumes section ensures that the application's memory persists. Just as the human mind retains experiences, Docker volumes store data, ensuring its longevity beyond the transient life of containers. Within the docker-compose.yml file, these volumes can be declared and then mounted to specific container paths. Such a mechanism ensures that databases retain their data, logs are accumulated, and configurations are preserved, even as containers are terminated and reborn.

However, the true genius of the docker-compose.yml file isn't just in its structural segments but in its declarative essence. By merely describing the desired state of the application, without delving into the operational specifics, developers can encapsulate complex architectures in a digestible format. With a simple docker-compose up, this textual blueprint metamorphoses into a living application, with Docker Compose handling the nuances of container creation, network establishment, and volume management.

Yet, like any powerful tool, the docker-compose.yml file demands respect and understanding. A misplaced attribute or an erroneous indentation can disrupt container orchestrated ballet. Developers must familiarize themselves with the official Docker Compose documentation, ensuring that their Compose files not only harness the full potential of Docker but also remain free of syntactical and logical pitfalls.

In conclusion, the docker-compose.yml file is the unsung hero of multi-container Docker applications. In its lines and indentations, it holds the power to define, deploy, and manage intricate software infrastructures. Translating the complex choreography of services, networks, and volumes into a clear, declarative script democratizes the orchestration process, inviting developers of all skill levels to embrace the magic of containerized applications. In the ever-evolving saga of Docker, the docker-compose.yml file stands tall, not merely as a chapter but as the binding thread weaving the narrative together.

Managing multi-container applications

In the vast cosmos of software development, we have witnessed a tectonic shift from monolithic architectures to microservices, a paradigm where each function of an application operates as an autonomous unit. As this approach gained traction, the landscape became dotted with many containers, each encapsulating a microservice. While this division promises scalability, flexibility, and resilience, it simultaneously introduces a new challenge: how to manage and orchestrate these myriad containers seamlessly? The tale of managing multi-container applications is akin to a conductor overseeing an orchestra, ensuring every instrument contributes harmoniously to the symphony.

To grapple with this intricate challenge, one must first understand the inherent complexity of multi-container applications. Unlike monoliths where components are tightly interwoven, microservices operate in relative isolation. Each service has its lifecycle, dependencies, and configuration. Moreover, they need to communicate, share data, and often, start in a specific sequence to ensure the application functions as intended. This multifaceted dance demands a sophisticated system to manage these containers, ensuring they coexist and cooperate seamlessly.

In its intrinsic wisdom, Docker presented a foundational solution by introducing containers—lightweight, standalone, and consistent units to package software. However, while Docker focused on individual containers, the real-world application often resembled an ensemble of these containers, each performing a unique role. Managing such a setup with manual Docker commands is feasible but hardly efficient. It's similar to tuning every instrument individually without a holistic view of the orchestra.

Enter container orchestration tools. These are the conductors of our metaphorical orchestra, offering a high-level mechanism to control and automate multiple containers' deployment, scaling, and management. Docker Compose, Kubernetes, and Docker Swarm emerge as the vanguards in this domain, each bringing its flavor to the orchestration feast.

Docker Compose stands out for developers keen on defining and running multi-container Docker applications. A simple YAML file can describe the entire application architecture, from services and networks to volumes. This configuration springs to life by executing docker-compose up, with Docker Compose handling the nitty-gritty of starting services in the correct order, establishing networks, and ensuring data persistence with volumes. Docker Compose emerges as a beacon of simplicity and efficiency for local development and testing.

However, when the spotlight shifts to production environments, especially those demanding high availability, scalability, and fault tolerance, Kubernetes and Docker Swarm take center stage. Kubernetes, often termed the gold standard of orchestration, offers a comprehensive platform to manage containerized workloads. With its pods, services, deployments, and ingress controllers, Kubernetes provides granular control over networking, scaling, load balancing, and rolling updates. Its ecosystem, rich with tools like Helm, Istio, and Prometheus, makes managing complex applications a structured endeavor, albeit with a steep learning curve.

Docker Swarm, on the other hand, offers a middle ground. As Docker's native clustering tool, Swarm focuses on simplicity and ease of use. With services, tasks, and stacks, Swarm ensures containers spread across multiple hosts, balancing load and recovering from failures. While it might lack Kubernetes' exhaustive feature set, its integration with the Docker ecosystem and straightforward commands make it a preferred choice for many looking to dip their toes into orchestration without being overwhelmed.

Regardless of the tool chosen, the core principles of managing multi-container applications remain consistent. First, always architect with failure in mind. In a distributed system, components will fail, but the system should recover gracefully. Tools like health checks, automated rollbacks, and self-healing mechanisms become pivotal. Second, ensure seamless communication. Service discovery, DNS resolution, and secure networking channels ensure that services talk to each other efficiently and securely. Lastly, monitor and log relentlessly. Visibility into the application's operations is crucial. Tools like Grafana, Fluentd, and ELK Stack provide insights, aiding in proactive issue resolution and optimization.

In the grand narrative of software evolution, multi-container applications mark a monumental chapter, echoing the industry's aspirations for modular, scalable, and resilient architectures. Yet, as with any masterpiece, the brilliance isn't just in individual notes but in their collective melody. Managing multi-container applications is about understanding this melody and harnessing orchestration tools to ensure each container and service contributes harmoniously. As developers and operators, our role mirrors that of the conductor— wielding the baton, guiding the orchestra, and crafting symphonies that resonate with perfection.

Chapter V

Docker Networking

Types of Docker Networks: bridge, host, overlay, none

The majestic realm of containerization, led by Docker, has bestowed the tech fraternity with tools that revolutionized how we perceive, develop, and deploy software. Containers, in their encapsulated splendor, provide consistent, reproducible, and isolated environments. However, as solitary as a container might seem, its real power unfolds when it communicates — with other containers, external applications, or the host machine. In this very act of communication, the unsung hero of the Docker ecosystem emerges: Docker Networking. Four primary types of Docker networks—bridge, host, overlay, and none—each offer distinct avenues for container communication, catering to diverse needs and scenarios. In this section, we shall journey through these intricate webs, understanding their nuances, applications, and intricacies.

Let us initiate our exploration with the default and perhaps the most commonly utilized Docker network: the bridge network. Imagine a bustling city, with each household representing a container. While every household has its own private affairs, they communicate with the external world through roads and bridges. The bridge network in

Docker mirrors this infrastructure. When a container is spawned without any specific network configuration, it attaches itself to this default bridge, having its private internal IP address. The bridge, acting as the mediator, facilitates the container's communication with the outside world, including other containers. However, to communicate, two containers under the bridge network must explicitly expose and map ports, similar to defining specific routes in our city analogy. While the bridge network is impeccable for single-host scenarios, especially during development, its limitations surface when multi-host communication is required or when a more granular network control is desired.

This leads us to the host network. In a departure from the bridge model, a container attached to the host network eschews the middle layer and binds directly to the host's IP stack. Drawing from our city analogy, if the bridge network implies individual households, the host network implies a communal living setup. Every container perceives the network as the host, with no internal IP segregation. This setup offers performance advantages, as there's no intermediary layer. It's particularly beneficial for applications that demand high-performance networking. However, this approach comes with a caveat. The direct binding implies a shared port namespace; hence, no two containers can bind to the same port on the host. Blurring boundaries between the container and host network also raises potential security concerns.

As organizations embraced Docker for larger deployments spanning multiple hosts, the need for a robust multi-host networking solution became palpable. Introducing the overlay network. If our earlier analogies resonated with urban setups, the overlay network is the equivalent of an interconnected highway system linking multiple cities. Created in the swarm mode, the overlay network allows containers across different hosts to communicate as if they resided on the same host. It achieves this feat through encapsulation, creating a virtual layer that sits atop the host's physical network. When deployed on this network, Swarm services can seamlessly discover and interact with each other, irrespective of their host machine. Moreover, built-in service discovery ensures that services can reach each other through aliases, abstracting the underlying container complexities. While the overlay network is a marvel for orchestrating multi-container, multi-host applications, it does introduce a slight latency due to its encapsulation mechanism.

Lastly, we touch upon the minimalist of all Docker networks: the none network. Stripping away all networking capabilities, this network type attaches a container to a network stack with no interfaces. In our city analogy, it's similar to a remote house, entirely cut off from external interactions. In this setup, the container becomes an isolated entity, unable to communicate externally. While this might seem counterintuitive, it serves specific use cases. For instance, when a container's sole purpose is to perform computational tasks using local resources without any external dependencies or interactions, the none network ensures that it operates in a completely isolated, distraction-free environment.

Navigating the Docker networking landscape requires a discerning understanding of application requirements. While the bridge network serves as a reliable default for single-host applications, the host network appeals to scenarios demanding performance sans intermediaries. With its expansive horizon, the overlay network empowers multi-host deployments, making it a darling of Docker Swarm setups. Conversely, in its simple approach, the none network champions complete isolation.

In conclusion, Docker, in its visionary approach, recognizes that networking isn't a one-size-fits-all paradigm. Just as the tapestry of global communication spans diverse mediums—from intimate letters to global satellite systems—container communication necessitates varied channels. The bridge, host, overlay, and none networks are Docker's testament to this diversity, each echoing a unique story of connection, isolation, and interaction. As developers and architects, our mission is to discern these narratives, choosing the network type that resonates perfectly with our application's symphony, ensuring that while our containers might operate in isolation, they never truly stand alone.

Inter-container communication

In the intricate ballet of modern software applications, individual components no longer dance solo; they perform in perfect synchrony, exchanging information, delegating tasks, and collaborating to present a cohesive show. The world of Docker containers, a microcosm of this larger paradigm, embodies this ethos profoundly. Containers, though designed to be independent, modular units, often need to communicate—to exchange data, synchronize processes, or distribute tasks. The ability of these containers to engage in intricate dialogues, or inter-container communication, is pivotal to the success of many contemporary software solutions. As we delve deeper into the art and science of these dialogues, it becomes clear that they are not just technical exchanges but harmonious orchestrations that echo the broader collaborative spirit of the digital age.

The fundamental premise behind Docker containers is isolation. Each container encapsulates its environment, ensuring that software runs uniformly regardless of where it is deployed. But, as any seasoned technologist will attest, applications seldom operate in isolation. They are parts of larger ecosystems, constantly interacting with other components. Thus, efficient communication becomes imperative when multiple containers need to cooperate, be it on the same host or distributed across a cluster.

A primary avenue for this inter-container discourse is the Docker network. By default, when a container is instantiated, it connects to a private internal network known as the bridge network. This network's container can seamlessly communicate, translating internal IP addresses and ports into a recognizable dialogue. However, this default configuration is not without its constraints. For one, direct communication between two containers on different hosts becomes challenging. Also, explicit port mappings are required to enable communication between a container and an external entity, adding a layer of complexity.

Docker offers various networking modes to overcome these limitations and enable more intricate container interactions. The host networking mode, for instance, binds a container directly to the host's network, eliminating any mediation. This direct binding facilitates high-speed communication but merges the container and host network namespaces, posing potential port conflicts. The overlay network, a more sophisticated model, shines in multi-host scenarios. Containers across different hosts perceive themselves as part of a single network, communicating transparently without any awareness of the underlying host distribution. While introducing a minor latency due to data encapsulation, this abstraction provides a powerful platform for orchestrating large-scale, distributed container applications.

Yet, network configurations are just the beginning. Beyond the fundamental network setup, inter-container communication often demands more nuanced patterns, especially when containers encapsulate microservices in a larger application ecosystem. Here, service discovery becomes paramount. Service discovery ensures that containers recognize and locate each other dynamically, adjusting to the fluid nature of containerized deployments where instances might be created, terminated, or moved frequently. Tools like Consul, etcd, and ZooKeeper, integrated with load balancers like HAProxy or Nginx, enable this dynamic container discovery and routing, ensuring that the dialogue remains uninterrupted despite changing container landscapes.

However, while service discovery addresses the 'where' of inter-container communication, the 'how' is equally crucial. How containers communicate, the protocols they employ, the data formats they recognize, and the security measures they adhere to, all define the quality and efficiency of their interaction. API-driven communication, predominantly over HTTP/REST or gRPC, becomes standard. These protocols, combined with data serialization formats like JSON or Protocol Buffers, ensure that container dialogues are efficient and standardized, fostering interoperability.

Security, the often overlooked but crucial aspect of inter-container dialogue, cannot be overstated. As containers engage in intimate exchanges, potentially transmitting sensitive data or critical commands, ensuring these communications are secure is pivotal. Transport Layer Security (TLS), employed with robust authentication and authorization mechanisms, fortifies these dialogues. Networks can further be segmented using Docker's network policies, ensuring that only authorized containers can initiate or accept communications, adding another layer of defense.

In conclusion, inter-container communication is not merely a technical orchestration; it mirrors the larger narrative of our interconnected digital world. As global systems—from financial markets to social networks—rely on seamless, secure, and efficient information exchanges, so do Docker containers. They might be isolated units, but their true potential, like individual notes in a symphony, unfolds in collaboration. Through networks, service discovery, communication protocols, and security measures, these containers engage in harmonious dialogues, underpinning the intricate dance of modern applications. As we architect, develop, and deploy in this containerized age, recognizing, facilitating, and optimizing these dialogues becomes our solemn duty—a duty that ensures our software not only functions but truly communicates.

Exposing services and ports

In the vast landscape of containerized deployments, the Docker container is a formidable entity, encapsulating and isolating environments to ensure that software runs consistently, irrespective of where it's deployed. But isolation, while one of its defining strengths, can also be an Achilles' heel. If a container remains wholly isolated, the software within remains an inaccessible enigma, unable to serve its purpose. This is where the subtle art of exposing services and ports comes into play, as the bridge connecting these isolated islands to the vast ocean of interactions in the digital realm.

To appreciate the essence of exposing services and ports, one must first grasp the anatomy of a container's network interface. A container, by its very nature, runs in a separate network namespace. This means it has its IP address, a set of network interfaces, and its routing table. While this encapsulation ensures the container's environment remains consistent, it also means that by default, the container cannot communicate with the external world, including the host on which it's running. This is where ports, the designated endpoints for network communication, become instrumental.

In its most basic form, exposing ports in Docker is a two-fold process: the declaration and the binding. The declaration, usually defined in a Dockerfile using the EXPOSE instruction, signifies that the software inside the container will be listening on the certain port(s). However, this alone does not make the service accessible. The stated port must be bound to a port on the host machine during container running in order to accomplish that. This binding effectively maps a port on the host to a port on the container, forming a bridge for communication.

But why is this mapping so crucial? Imagine a bustling harbor with numerous isolated islands (containers) floating on a vast sea (the host machine). Each island has private docks (ports) to receive ships (data packets). For the mainland (external world) to send or access goods from an island, they need to know which dock to approach. Exposing and binding ports is akin to assigning specific docks on the mainland to particular islands, ensuring seamless and directed communication.

The utility of exposing services extends beyond mere communication. In a microservices architecture, where an application is broken down into smaller, modular services, each running in its container, the exposure of services becomes the backbone of the application's functionality. By selectively exposing and binding ports, one can dictate the flow of communication between these services, ensuring that they interact cohesively while maintaining their encapsulated environments.

However, exposing services and ports is not without its challenges and considerations. A primary concern is security. Every exposed port is a potential entry point for malicious entities. Hence, exposing only the necessary ports and adhering to safety best practices becomes paramount. Techniques like employing firewalls to filter incoming and outgoing traffic, using Transport Layer Security (TLS) to encrypt data in transit, and regularly scanning containers for vulnerabilities are essential measures to fortify exposed services.

Another pivotal consideration is port conflicts. Since a host machine has limited ports, binding multiple containers to the same host port can result in conflicts. Efficient port management, potentially employing dynamic port assignments, can alleviate this issue. Moreover, tools like Docker Compose can be instrumental in defining multi-container applications with intricate service exposures, ensuring that port assignments are consistent and conflict-free.

Beyond these technical considerations, there's a philosophical aspect to exposing services and ports. In many ways, the process mirrors the broader narrative of openness and collaboration in the digital era. Just as technologies, platforms, and communities have embraced open standards, interfaces, and APIs to foster collaboration, containers, through exposed ports, open themselves up to the world. They break out of their isolated shells, inviting interactions, and in the process, become part of larger, interconnected ecosystems.

In conclusion, the process of exposing services and ports in containerized environments is a dance of technical precision and philosophical openness. It recognizes that while isolation ensures consistency, communication is the lifeblood of functionality. As containers dominate the software deployment landscape, understanding and mastering the art of service exposure becomes vital. Through these exposed ports and services, containers, much like bustling islands in a vast digital ocean, engage with the world, facilitating the harmonious symphony of modern software interactions.

Chapter VI

Persistent Storage in Docker

Docker Volumes vs Bind Mounts

In the sprawling narrative of containerized architectures, where applications are encapsulated in ephemeral vessels, data persistence becomes intriguing and imperative. While the transient nature of containers offers deployment agility and environmental consistency, it also poses a problem: how does one ensure that data survives beyond the fleeting life of a container? Introducing Docker Volumes and Bind Mounts, two protagonists in Docker's tale of data persistence. As we venture into their duel, we uncover their technical distinctions and philosophical approaches to handling data in the containerized cosmos.

At a foundational level, both Docker Volumes and Bind Mounts address the same fundamental challenge: ensuring that data within a container can be stored in a manner that outlives the container's lifecycle. But the paths they tread, the mechanisms they employ, and the scenarios they cater to, diverge, painting two distinct narratives of data persistence.

In many ways, Docker Volumes are the native heroes of Docker's persistence saga. Crafted explicitly to store container data, volumes exist as independent entities on the host filesystem. Their creation, management, and deletion are orchestrated through Docker commands, ensuring their lifecycle is intuitive and integrated into the broader Docker experience. Volumes boast a decoupled architecture, meaning they don't mandatorily bind to any specific container. This decoupling ensures that even as containers are spawned, terminated, or migrated, the volume and precious data remains steadfast. Moreover, Docker volumes are inherently portable. They can be backed up, shared, or migrated across hosts, ensuring data consistency and accessibility across diverse deployment landscapes.

Furthermore, the versatility of Docker Volumes is accentuated by the pluggable nature of Docker's volume drivers. These drivers empower users to store data not just on the local filesystem, but across many storage solutions, from cloud-based storage like AWS EBS or Google Cloud Storage to network-based solutions like NFS. This extensibility, combined with the inherent resilience and lifecycle management capabilities of volumes, positions Docker Volumes as a robust, native solution for container data persistence.

Juxtaposed against this is the narrative of Bind Mounts, the seasoned veterans of the filesystem world, adapted to the containerized context. Bind mounts are directories or files on the host system that are "mounted" into containers. They predate Docker and are rooted in the traditional Unix concept of mounting filesystems. When a directory from the host is bind-mounted into a container, any data written by the container to that mount point is, in reality, written to the host's directory, ensuring data persistence beyond the container's existence. Given their legacy, bind mounts offer a familiar paradigm for those well-versed with traditional filesystem operations.

But with this legacy comes a set of considerations. Bind mounts, being directories on the host system, are tightly coupled to the host's directory structure. This coupling implies that the host's directory structure and permissions become crucial determinants of the bind mount's behavior. Moreover, the inherent portability that Docker volumes boast of is not native to bind mounts. Since bind mounts are tied to specific directories on specific hosts, replicating or migrating containers across hosts demands manual orchestration to ensure data consistency.

Yet, despite these considerations, bind mounts shine in scenarios where direct access to the host's filesystem is essential. For developers looking to containerize applications during development phases, bind mounts offer an agile mechanism to reflect code changes in real-time within the container, without needing continuous rebuilds. They also cater to situations where existing data or directory structures on the host must be seamlessly integrated into the container's operational realm.

In Docker's grand spectrum of data persistence, volumes and bind mounts represent two facets of the same intent. While Docker volumes, with their decoupled architecture, native lifecycle management, and extensible storage backends, cater to scenarios demanding robustness and portability, bind mounts, with their direct access to the host filesystem and real-time data reflection, serve use cases rooted in agility and direct host integration.

In conclusion, the duel between Docker Volumes and Bind Mounts is less about superiority and more about suitability. In the intricate ballet of containerized deployments, they dance not as adversaries but as partners, each stepping in when their unique strengths align with the demands of the narrative. For architects, developers, and operators, understanding their nuances is less about choosing a victor and more about orchestrating a harmonious performance, where data, despite the transience of containers, finds its persistent stage.

Managing data persistence

In the grand theater of modern software deployments, Docker containers have emerged as the actors that encapsulate applications in consistently replicable environments. But, like actors who play their roles and exit the stage, containers are inherently ephemeral. They appear, perform their duties, and then dissipate, leaving no trace. While advantageous for ensuring environmental purity and agility, this transience poses a significant challenge when faced with data's innate desire for permanence. How does one ensure that amidst the fleeting performances of containers, data finds its enduring sanctum? The quest for managing data persistence in Docker explores this very question—a journey where technology meets philosophy.

In the Docker ecosystem, the gravitas of this question becomes evident when one appreciates the essential dichotomy of data and application state. While application code can be containerized, executed, and disposed of without any lasting consequences, data demands continuity, especially in stateful applications. A user's preferences, a database's records, or an application's logs—these data fragments, if lost, disrupt the narrative of user experiences and application functionality. Therefore, as we deploy applications in Docker containers, ensuring that the data they generate and manipulate persists beyond the container's lifecycle becomes paramount.

At the heart of Docker's approach to data persistence lies the concept of volumes. These are specially crafted entities within the Docker realm, designed to offer a sanctuary for data amidst the transient world of containers. Volumes exist on the host filesystem, independent of the container's life, and can be simultaneously attached to one or more containers. This attachment ensures that any data written to the volume from within the container gets stored on the host, safe from the ephemeral winds of container termination. The lifecycle of these volumes, from their creation to their deletion, is governed through Docker commands, ensuring that data management remains integrated within the Docker workflow. Moreover, with their decoupled architecture, volumes can be backed up, shared, or migrated, offering flexibility in how data is accessed and preserved.

Supplementing this narrative is Docker's support for bind mounts. Rooted in traditional Unix filesystem operations, bind mounts allow specific directories or files on the host system to be mounted into containers. While similar in principle to volumes, bind mounts cater to scenarios demanding direct, real-time access to the host's filesystem. They serve as conduits, reflecting changes on the host into the container and vice-versa, making them particularly useful in development environments where code or configuration changes need to be instantly mirrored within running containers.

However, managing data persistence in Docker isn't just about understanding the technicalities of volumes and bind mounts. It's about the broader philosophy of data stewardship in containerized environments. As with any technology, there are caveats and considerations to be acknowledged.

Firstly, there's the challenge of data integrity. In a world where containers can be rapidly spawned and terminated, ensuring that concurrent writes or reads to shared volumes do not corrupt data is vital. Mechanisms like locking or single-writer policies can be employed to ensure data integrity.

Then there's the consideration of data security. While facilitating data persistence, every volume or bind mount also opens up potential avenues for data breaches. Ensuring volumes are encrypted, enforcing strict access controls, and regularly auditing data access patterns become foundational practices in Docker's data management realm.

The conversation around data persistence also extends into the broader ecosystem of tools and platforms that integrate with Docker. Platforms like Kubernetes, which orchestrate multi-container deployments, introduce their constructs like Persistent Volumes and

Persistent Volume Claims, further expanding the horizons of data management in containerized deployments.

Moreover, as we navigate the Docker data landscape, the importance of regular backups and disaster recovery mechanisms becomes evident. While volumes and bind mounts ensure data persistence across container lifecycles, they do not inherently guarantee data durability against system failures or accidental deletions. Employing regular backup strategies, coupled with tested recovery mechanisms, fortifies the sanctuary of data in the Docker world.

The quest for managing data persistence in Docker is a voyage that oscillates between the technical and the philosophical. It's a narrative where the tools and techniques, like volumes and bind mounts, intertwine with the broader ideologies of data stewardship, security, and integrity. As Docker continues redefining software deployment paradigms, ensuring that data finds its persistent home amidst the ephemeral choreography of containers becomes both an art and a science. And as architects, developers, and operators, navigating this delicate balance ensures that even in the fleeting performances of containers, the stories etched in data endure, timeless and uninterrupted.

Backing up and restoring data

In the evolving landscape of software deployment and execution, Docker has illuminated the path with its ability to house applications in neatly defined, consistently replicable containers. However, with the adoption of such modern, ephemeral container architectures comes the age-old challenge magnified: safeguarding the persistent tales of data amidst the changing actors of containers. Like preserving ancient manuscripts through the ravages of time, backing up and restoring data in Docker becomes a foundational pillar, ensuring that our data stories remain intact, even as containers rise and fall in their transient dance.

Understanding the significance of data backup and restoration in Docker starts by appreciating the inherent ephemerality of containers. These units, by design, are transient; they can be started, stopped, deleted, and recreated easily. While this nature is advantageous for scalability and deployment purity, it accentuates the vulnerability of data generated and managed by these containers. If a container is removed, the data within its writable layer might disappear into oblivion, unless it's safeguarded within Docker volumes or bind mounts. But even then, what guarantees the sanctity of this data against accidental deletions, system failures, or unanticipated corruptions? This realization ignites the quest for robust backup and restoration strategies.

Docker Volumes are the primary custodians of persistent data within the Docker universe. These entities, residing on the host file system, are isolated from the containers' ephemeral lifecycle. When considering backup strategies, Docker volumes naturally become the focal point. The most straightforward approach involves copying data from the volume to an external backup location using traditional file system tools. Commands like tar can be used to create an archive of the volume's data, which can then be stored in backup systems, be they on-premises storage or cloud-based solutions. For instance, backing up a volume might involve running a container to create a tar archive of the volume's content, which can subsequently be transferred to a backup location.

The beauty of this backup method is its universality; the generated backup is agnostic to Docker and can be restored even in non-Dockerized environments. However, the same universality also means that the backup process doesn't inherently capture the metadata or the nuances associated with the Docker volume, making restoration a meticulous task.

However, Docker's ever-evolving ecosystem also boasts tools that offer more sophisticated backup solutions. Utilities and platforms integrate directly with Docker's API to facilitate backups that preserve data and retain volume configurations, metadata, and nuances. These tools can automate backups, ensuring consistent snapshots of volumes, and can integrate with popular storage solutions, allowing backups to be seamlessly stored and managed in diverse environments.

Restoration, the counterpart of the backup narrative, is both an art and a science. At its core, restoring data involves repopulating a Docker volume from a backup. For backups created using traditional filesystem tools, the restoration process might involve creating a new volume and then populating it using commands like tar to extract data from the backup archive. However, in scenarios where backups were created using specialized Docker tools, the restoration might involve using the same toolset, which can recreate the volume with all its configurations, ensuring that the restored environment mirrors the original.

Yet, while the technicalities of backup and restoration processes are paramount, the philosophy surrounding them is equally significant. Backup strategies need regular validation. It's not uncommon for organizations to religiously back up data, only to realize during a crisis that the backups are corrupted, outdated, or missing critical data. Thus, periodically testing the restoration process, simulating disaster scenarios, and validating the integrity of the backup data is essential.

Furthermore, the cadence of backups is a critical consideration. How frequently should data be backed up? The answer isn't universal and hinges on the application's nature, the data change rate, and the data loss tolerance. For some mission-critical applications, incremental backups might be performed every few hours, while daily snapshots might suffice for others.

In conclusion, the narrative of backing up and restoring data in Docker is a testament to the timeless importance of data preservation, even in the modern, fluid world of containerization. It's a tale that reminds us that while technology evolves, the essence of specific challenges remains consistent. As Docker containers redefine software execution paradigms, the rituals of backing up and restoring data stand as sentinels, ensuring that the stories scripted in bytes and bits remain eternal, transcending the temporal boundaries of container lifecycles. It's a dance of preservation, where technology and intent waltz in harmony, safeguarding tales against the relentless march of time.

Chapter VII

Docker Swarm:
Native Clustering for Docker

Understanding Swarm mode

In the software world, as applications scale and grow, an intricate ballet of managing, coordinating, and scaling containerized services arises. While Docker's inception revolutionized how applications are packaged and run, the challenges of overseeing a plethora of containers, ensuring their seamless interaction, and guaranteeing high availability have given rise to another dimension in container management: orchestration. In Docker's expansive universe, this orchestration is epitomized by the "Swarm mode," a native clustering and scheduling tool that transforms individual Docker engines into a cohesive, self-organizing fleet, aptly termed a "swarm."

To truly grasp the essence of Swarm mode, one must first delve into the motivations behind its inception. The world of containerized applications is wider than solitary containers running in isolation. More often than not, modern applications comprise multiple services, each potentially replicated across several containers for load distribution and redundancy. Ensuring these services discover each other, communicate seamlessly, handle failures, and scale in response to demand is non-trivial. This complexity gave birth to the orchestration paradigm, and within Docker's domain, Swarm mode emerged as the native solution to these challenges.

At its heart, Swarm mode is a distributed system that provides a declarative approach to defining desired application states. Instead of manual interventions to deploy or scale services, developers describe their intent—how many replicas of a service should run, what networks they should connect to, or which data volumes they should use. Swarm mode then takes on the responsibility of realizing this intent, deciding where to run containers, how to load-balance traffic, or what to do when nodes or services fail.

The underpinnings of Swarm mode lie in its architecture. In Docker parlance, a swarm is a collection of Docker nodes, which can be either managers or workers. Manager nodes are the custodians of the swarm's control plane. They maintain the swarm's state, make scheduling decisions, and, critically, manage the swarm's consensus algorithm to ensure consistency across the cluster. In contrast, worker nodes are the foot soldiers, executing containers as commanded by the manager nodes. This separation of responsibilities ensures both operational efficiency and resilicnce. Even if a few nodes, be they managers or workers, face failures, the swarm can continue its operations unperturbed.

One of Swarm mode's distinguishing features is its in-built service discovery mechanism. As services are deployed and scaled within a swarm, they are automatically assigned DNS names and can discover other services using these names. This capability, coupled with load balancing, ensures that inter-service communications are seamless, efficient, and fault-tolerant.

Yet, Swarm mode isn't merely a technical solution; it embodies a philosophy. Its design choices prioritize simplicity and ease of use. Setting up a swarm, adding or removing nodes, or deploying services, is achieved with simple Docker commands. There's no need for external databases or discovery backends. Everything required for orchestrating containers is encapsulated within the Docker engines participating in the swarm.

However, understanding Swarm mode also entails recognizing its position in the broader orchestration landscape. While Swarm mode excels in its simplicity and tight integration with Docker, the world of container orchestration isn't monolithic. Tools like Kubernetes have carved significant mindshare, offering a feature-rich ecosystem for complex use cases. This diversity has often led to debates and comparisons, with Swarm mode being lauded for its simplicity and ease of setup, while Kubernetes is often chosen for more complex, enterprise-grade deployments.

In conclusion, Swarm mode is Docker's poetic expression of container orchestration—a ballet director ensuring that each container and service dances in harmony, scales with grace, and recovers with elegance. It's a testament to Docker's vision of providing tools to run applications and manage, scale, and secure them. As developers and operators, diving deep into Swarm mode offers insights into the nuances of container orchestration, the challenges of distributed systems, and the beauty of declarative application management. While the orchestration landscape is vast and varied, Swarm mode is a beacon for those seeking a native, simple, yet powerful solution to choreograph their container ballet. In the grand performance of modern software, with containers playing their parts, Swarm mode emerges as the maestro, orchestrating, guiding, and ensuring that the show goes on, irrespective of failures, scale, or complexity.

Setting up a Swarm cluster

In the sprawling realms of software, the heart of innovation often beats to the rhythm of scalability, reliability, and efficiency. Docker, a transformative force in containerization, magnified these tenets by offering an abstraction that allowed applications to be encapsulated in consistent, portable, and efficient containers. Yet, the narrative evolved as these applications matured and grew complex, spanning multiple services and demanding higher availability. The answer wasn't just to run containers but to orchestrate them, to manage their dance, to ensure their harmonious interactions, and to guarantee their continuous performance. Introducing the Swarm mode, Docker's native orchestration solution. And at its core, the Swarm cluster, a coalition of Docker nodes, stands as the stage on which this orchestration unfolds. Setting up this cluster, therefore, becomes akin to setting the stage for a grand symphony of containerized services.

To venture into the odyssey of setting up a Swarm cluster, one must first grasp the essence of its components. At a fundamental level, a Swarm cluster is composed of Docker nodes. These nodes, the individual machines (be they physical servers or virtual instances) running the Docker daemon, wear two primary hats: Manager and Worker. Manager nodes are the conductors of our container symphony. They hold the blueprints, the service definitions, the desired states, and orchestrate the overall dance of the containers. They are responsible for the intricate decisions: where to run a container, how to respond to a node's failure, or when to scale a service. In contrast, Worker nodes, true to their name, are the workhorses, running the containers, executing the tasks, and rendering the services. This division of labor contradiction ensures that the Swarm cluster operates efficiently, balancing the demands of decision-making with the imperatives of execution.

Initiating this cluster begins with a foundational act: initializing the Swarm on a Docker node. By running the command docker swarm init, a Docker node metamorphoses into a Manager node, birthing a new Swarm. This initialization act creates a series of cryptographic artifacts, ensuring secure node-to-node communication and generating a unique token, which will subsequently be the key for other nodes to join this nascent swarm. With this, the cornerstone of the Swarm cluster is laid, and the orchestration journey begins.

With a manager in place, the next step is to grow the swarm, to invite nodes into this orchestrated collective. Using the token generated during initialization, other Docker nodes can be beckoned into the swarm using the docker swarm join command. Depending on the token used, these nodes either join as managers or workers. It's essential to underscore the significance of this choice. While it might be tempting to have multiple manager nodes (for high availability), one must tread cautiously. Manager nodes, being the decision-makers, use a consensus algorithm to maintain a consistent view of the swarm. Having too many managers can slow down this consensus process. Therefore, a balance must be struck, typically adhering to odd numbers like three or five managers for medium to large deployments.

The cluster starts taking shape as the nodes join the swarm, but it's not just about numbers. It's about connectivity, resilience, and security. Each node in the swarm communicates over encrypted channels, ensuring that service orchestration happens securely. The Swarm mode also takes care of service discovery and load balancing. As services are defined and deployed, they are automatically assigned virtual IP addresses, allowing seamless inter-service communication. The manager nodes, with their in-built load balancers, also ensure that incoming requests to a service are efficiently distributed among its task instances.

Yet, setting up a Swarm cluster isn't confined to initializing and joining nodes. It's an ongoing commitment to monitoring, scaling, and managing. Nodes might need to be promoted from workers to managers or demoted in the opposite direction. They might need to be drained for maintenance, ensuring no new tasks are scheduled. Or, in unfortunate circumstances, nodes might need to be removed from the swarm. While available as Docker commands, each of these operations demands thoughtfulness, ensuring that the swarm's integrity, performance, and resilience are always upheld.

Furthermore, in a world where infrastructure is as fluid as software, where servers can be spun up in cloud environments in a matter of minutes, Swarm clusters also embrace dynamicity. They can be integrated with cloud provider APIs, allowing the swarm to be aware of underlying infrastructure changes, and to adapt, scale, or recover accordingly.

In conclusion, setting up a Swarm cluster is a journey, an expedition into the world of orchestration, where individual Docker nodes come together, shedding their isolated identities, and become part of a larger, orchestrated collective. It's not just about running commands; it's about understanding the underlying principles, the division of responsibilities, the imperatives of secure communication, and the nuances of service discovery and load balancing. It's about choreographing a symphony, where each Docker container and service plays its part, but always in harmony, always in rhythm with others. As our software ecosystems evolve, demanding more scalability, resilience, and dynamism, Swarm clusters emerge as the beacon, illuminating the path to effective, efficient, and elegant orchestration. It's a testament to Docker's vision, where the focus isn't just on creating containers but orchestrating their dance, ensuring that the show goes on, gracefully, powerfully, and reliably.

Deploying services in Swarm mode

In the majestic panorama of software evolution, Docker's emergence as a champion of containerization marked a pivotal inflection point. Containers brought the promise of consistency, portability, and isolation, rendering applications as self-sufficient entities capable of running anywhere. Yet, as these applications burgeoned in complexity and size, a new challenge arose: How do you efficiently manage, coordinate, and scale a vast sea of containers, mainly when they're scattered across multiple machines or even data centers? Introducing Swarm mode, Docker's native orchestration mechanism, designed to conduct the intricate ballet of containers in a distributed environment. At the heart of this orchestration lies the concept of services, a higher-level abstraction over containers, representing a specific task or role within a distributed application. Deploying services in Swarm mode, thus, becomes the art and science of defining, scaling, and managing these roles, ensuring that the holistic application performs seamlessly, efficiently, and resiliently.

Understanding service deployment in Swarm mode necessitates a deep dive into the concept of a service. At its essence, a service in Docker's lexicon describes a desired state. Rather than focusing on running individual containers, when deploying a service, one articulates the intent: How many instances (or replicas) of a particular containerized task should run? What network should they be connected to? Which volumes should they access? What policy should guide their update or rollback? This declarative approach liberates developers and operators from the minutiae of container management, allowing them to focus on defining the application's behavior and letting Swarm mode handle the orchestration.

Embarking on the journey of deploying a service in Swarm mode begins with the docker service create command. This command, rich in options and parameters, allows one to define the service's blueprint. From specifying the container image to use, setting environment variables, defining network connections, to even stipulating resource limits and reservations, docker service create is the architect's tool, enabling the precise definition of a service's behavior and constraints. Once executed, the Swarm manager nodes swing into action, scheduling the specified number of tasks (container instances) as per the service's definition. These tasks are intelligently placed across the swarm's nodes, considering resource availability, existing service constraints, and node affinities or anti-affinities.

Yet, the lifecycle of a service isn't static; it's a dynamic entity that might need to evolve as application requirements change. Swarm mode understands this dynamism, offering a suite of management commands to modify a service post-deployment. For instance, the docker service update command empowers one to scale the service, change its image, add or remove network connections, or even update its configuration. This command ensures that changes are applied gracefully, with minimal disruption, following defined update policies. Rolling updates, where a few tasks are updated at a time, can be configured, ensuring the service remains available even during upgrades.

Scaling a service, adjusting its replica count to meet changing demands, is a frequent operation. Swarm mode simplifies this with the docker service scale command, allowing rapid scaling up or down, with the swarm's manager nodes recalibrating task distribution accordingly. This elastic scalability ensures applications can handle varying loads gracefully, without manual intervention.

Another nuanced facet of deploying services in Swarm mode is network connectivity. Services often need to communicate, discover each other, and sometimes expose their functionality to external entities. Swarm mode's in-built DNS service ensures that services can address each other by name, making inter-service communication straightforward. Furthermore, services can be attached to overlay networks, ensuring that tasks of a service, even if running on different nodes, can communicate as if on the same local network. For services that need to be accessible externally, Swarm mode provides the ingress load balancer, distributing incoming requests to service tasks, irrespective of the node they land on.

Service deployment in Swarm mode isn't just about creation and management; it's also about introspection. Commands like docker service ps or docker service logs provide insights into a service's health, task distribution, and runtime behavior. This introspection is crucial, ensuring operators can monitor, troubleshoot, and optimize service performance.

In conclusion, deploying services in Swarm mode is a transformative experience. It moves the focus from individual containers to holistic service definitions, from imperatively running tasks to declaratively defining desired states. It's an orchestration ballet, where services, each representing a specific role or function, dance in harmony, communicate with grace, scale with agility, and recover with resilience. As distributed applications become the norm, the need for robust, efficient, and intuitive orchestration mechanisms becomes paramount. Swarm mode rises to this occasion, offering a native, integrated, and powerful orchestration solution. Deploying services within it is not just a technical operation; it's an embrace of a philosophy where applications are defined by their behavior, interactions, and responses to changing environments. In the grand tapestry of modern software, where microservices play their parts, Swarm mode stands as the conductor, ensuring the symphony plays on, beautifully, harmoniously, and resiliently.

Chapter VIII

Docker Security Best Practices

Running containers securely

With Docker at its forefront, the meteoric rise of containerization has fundamentally reshaped the landscape of software development and deployment. As the allure of containers has grown, they have been rapidly adopted by organizations of all sizes, lauded for their promise of consistency, portability, and scalability. But as with all technological advancements, the shift to containerized environments has brought forth a new set of challenges—chief among them is the need for secure operations. In a world of escalating cyber threats, ensuring the safe execution of containers is of paramount importance. This pursuit of security encompasses a broad spectrum, ranging from the integrity of container images to runtime isolation, network policies, and beyond.

The foundation of secure container operations begins with a principle as old as computing itself: the principle of least privilege. This principle dictates that a process (in this case, a container) should only be granted the permissions that are absolutely essential for its operation, and no more. Docker inherently embraces this principle by isolating container processes from each other and from the host system using a combination of Linux namespaces, control groups (cgroups), and Mandatory Access Controls (MAC) like AppArmor and SELinux. These mechanisms collectively ensure that even if malicious actors compromise a container, their ability to inflict damage or escalate their privileges remains constrained.

Yet, the principle of least privilege extends beyond just process isolation. It seeps into how container images are built and sourced. The images form the blueprint from which containers are instantiated, and their integrity is crucial. Relying on trusted base images, sourced from reputable repositories, ensures that the software stack within the container starts from a foundation of trust. Tools like Docker Content Trust further cement this trust by enabling image signing and verification, ensuring that images haven't been tampered with during transit. Additionally, regular scanning of container images for vulnerabilities, and the subsequent patching or updating of these images, acts as a proactive measure, nipping potential security threats in the bud.

While image integrity forms the bedrock of secure container operations, the runtime environment's configuration is equally vital. A hardened container runtime configuration limits potential attack vectors. For instance, Docker allows dropping unnecessary Linux capabilities, ensuring that containers don't have unwarranted system privileges. Running containers as non-root users further limits the blast radius should a container be breached. Additionally, resource constraints, set using cgroups, prevent resource-exhaustion attacks, where a rogue container could potentially starve other containers or the host system of critical resources like CPU, memory, or I/O bandwidth.

Networking, the lifeblood of interconnected containerized applications, presents its own set of security considerations. Docker's network modes, such as bridge, host, and overlay, offer varying degrees of isolation and communication capabilities. For instance, the bridge mode, the default network mode, provides a private internal network on the host system, ensuring inter-container communication while keeping containers isolated from external networks. By utilizing network policies, one can finely tune the communication channels, allowing only necessary traffic between containers or services, effectively creating a firewall of sorts. Moreover, user-defined bridge networks or overlay networks in Swarm mode provide DNS resolution for containers, ensuring they can communicate using container names, a feature that simplifies secure container-to-container communication.

Storage, another cornerstone of containerized environments, especially when considering stateful applications, needs careful attention from a security perspective. Docker volumes, the preferred mechanism for persistent storage, can be secured using proper access controls, ensuring that only authorized containers can read or write data. Additionally, considering encrypted storage solutions can safeguard sensitive data, rendering it useless even if unauthorized access occurs.

Lastly, monitoring and auditing form the final layers of a comprehensive container security strategy. Tools and platforms that provide real-time monitoring capabilities allow for rapidly detecting abnormal behaviors. Coupled with extensive logging, both at the container and host levels, these tools facilitate the early detection of security incidents and aid in forensic analysis, helping trace back and understand the nature and source of threats.

In conclusion, while transformative, the shift to containerized environments comes with a heightened responsibility to ensure secure operations. Containers' ephemeral nature, dynamic life cycles, and intricate interactions present unique security challenges. Addressing these challenges needs a holistic approach, encompassing image integrity, runtime configurations, network and storage security, and proactive monitoring. As containers continue to permeate modern software infrastructures, the emphasis on running them securely will only intensify. And as it does, the principles and practices outlined above will serve as guiding beacons, ensuring that the myriad benefits of containerization are realized without compromising the sanctity and security of our digital assets.

Using Docker Secrets

The contemporary world of software development and deployment has witnessed a tectonic shift with the adoption of containerization. Docker, one of the pioneers in this domain, has been at the vanguard of this transformation. As businesses increasingly transition to container-based infrastructure, the importance of security in such ecosystems can't be understated. One critical aspect of this security paradigm involves managing sensitive information like the passwords, API keys, and tokens. Docker acknowledges this challenge and has proffered a solution like Docker Secrets, a mechanism designed to secure sensitive data in a Dockerized environment.

The core premise of Docker Secrets lies in its ability to provide a secure method to store and manage sensitive information. Traditional methods often involved hardcoding these secrets directly into images or code, using environment variables, or relying on external tools. These approaches, while functional, were fraught with vulnerabilities. Hardcoded secrets made images less reusable and exposed sensitive data to anyone accessing the image. Though a step in the right direction, environment variables could be inadvertently leaked in logs or exposed to linked containers. External tools added another layer of complexity and dependencies.

Docker Secrets emerged as a robust alternative to these methods, primarily geared towards Docker's Swarm mode, although it has applications beyond just Swarm. At its heart, Docker Secrets is a file-based mechanism. Secrets are stored in the Swarm's in-built Raft database, encrypted at rest, and transmitted securely between nodes using mutual TLS. This ensures that secrets are stored securely and remain secure during transit.

A remarkable facet of Docker Secrets is its simplicity of use. Creating a secret is as straightforward as using the 'docker secret create' command. Once created, this secret can be granted to services during their deployment. What's ingenious is how Docker handles the secret post-deployment. The secret isn't baked into the container image or left in an environment variable. Instead, it's mounted as a read-only file within the container, typically under the "/run/secrets/" directory. This approach ensures that only containers that need access to the secret can access it, and even within those containers, the exposure is minimal.

The lifecycle management of secrets is also a testament to Docker's commitment to security. Old or compromised secrets can be seamlessly rotated without causing undue disruption to running services. New secrets can be created, and services can be updated to use the more recent version. This ability to rotate secrets, combined with the principle of least privilege, ensures that the window of vulnerability remains limited even if a secret were to be compromised.

But as with all tools, Docker Secrets is not a silver bullet. While it provides robust security mechanisms, its effective utilization requires understanding its limitations. For instance, secrets are designed to be immutable. Once set, they cannot be directly modified. Changes necessitate the creation of a new version of the secret. Additionally, while Docker Secrets is primarily designed for Swarm mode, applications running outside this orchestration might require other solutions like Docker's credential helpers or third-party tools like HashiCorp's Vault.

Furthermore, organizations need to be aware of operational practices that might inadvertently compromise the efficacy of Docker Secrets. For instance, logging or debugging mechanisms that expose the file system or print environment details could unintentionally reveal the contents of the secrets. Developers and operations teams must be trained to be aware of such nuances, ensuring that integrating Docker Secrets into the CI/CD pipeline doesn't become a potential vulnerability.

In conclusion, Docker Secrets represents a significant stride in addressing the challenges of secret management in containerized environments. It melds simplicity with robustness, providing developers and operators with a tool that safeguards sensitive data and integrates seamlessly into their workflows. However, as is the case with all security tools, its strength lies not just in its technical prowess but in the awareness and practices of its users. Organizations adopting Docker Secrets must invest in educating their teams, establishing best practices, and continually monitoring and updating their approaches in line with the evolving threat landscape. In doing so, they ensure that Docker Secrets remains the bastion of security it's designed to be, safeguarding the sanctity of their data in the dynamic world of containerized applications.

Limiting container resources

The essence of containerization, epitomized by Docker, rests in its ability to provide isolated, reproducible, and scalable application environments. Containers share the host system's kernel but operate in isolated user spaces, ensuring minimal overhead and near-native performance. However, the very strengths of containers can become challenges in environments where multiple containers vie for system resources. Without proper controls, one container could monopolize system resources, adversely affecting other containers or even the host system itself. The solution lies in the judicious management and limitation of container resources, striking a balance that ensures optimal system performance and fairness.

The importance of resource limitation in containerized environments is multifaceted. At a primary level, it's about system stability and performance. If left unchecked, a runaway process within a container can consume an excessive amount of CPU, memory, or I/O bandwidth, leading to system instability or reduced performance for other applications. Moreover, in multi-tenant environments or cloud platforms where multiple users run containers on shared infrastructure, the absence of resource limitations can result in the proverbial "noisy neighbor" problem, where one user's containers degrade the performance of others.

Resource constraints in Docker and other container platforms are implemented using Linux's control groups, or cgroups. This kernel feature allows Docker to set limits and restrictions on CPU, memory, I/O, and network resources. With these controls in place, system administrators and operators can define the maximum resources a container can consume, ensuring that no single container can wreak havoc on the system.

CPU constraints are among the most commonly applied. Docker provides mechanisms to set both hard and soft limits on CPU resources. One can assign a relative weight to a container using CPU shares, ensuring it gets a proportionate share of the CPU cycles. Additionally, Docker permits setting specific CPU cores for containers, providing a more granular control. In scenarios where precise limits are required, Docker allows setting a quota on CPU cycles, ensuring that a container never uses more than a predefined number of cycles.

Memory management is another crucial aspect of resource limitation. Without proper memory constraints, a container with a memory leak or a process that suddenly consumes a vast amount of memory can lead to system-wide issues, including the dreaded out-of-memory (OOM) conditions. Docker provides options to set both memory and swap limits for containers. By defining a maximum memory usage, operators can ensure that a container is automatically restarted or stopped if it exceeds the set limit, preventing it from affecting the more extensive system.

While CPU and memory are the most discussed resources, I/O bandwidth and network throughput are equally vital, especially in data-intensive applications or services that involve substantial data transfers. Docker provides options to limit block I/O, which relates to disk access, and network I/O. Through these mechanisms, one can ensure that containers do not overwhelm disk drives with excessive read/write operations or flood network interfaces, thereby ensuring fairness and stability.

However, as beneficial as resource limitations are, they come with their own set of challenges. Setting constraints requires an in-depth understanding of application behavior and needs. Overly restrictive limits can adversely affect application performance as having no limits at all. It's a delicate dance of understanding the resource requirements of an application during its lifecycle, from idle periods to peak loads. Furthermore, static resource limits may need regular revisiting and adjustment in dynamic environments where workloads evolve.

This intricate balance of resource management underscores the importance of monitoring in containerized environments. Effective monitoring solutions can provide insights into container behavior, highlighting resource usage patterns, and indicating potential bottlenecks or inefficiencies. Such insights inform immediate resource allocation decisions and guide future container scaling and deployment strategies.

In conclusion, as containerization continues to dominate the software deployment landscape, the nuances of managing container resources become paramount. While containers promise isolation, reproducibility, and scalability, they operate in shared environments where resources are finite. Limiting container resources, using tools and mechanisms provided by platforms like Docker, is not just a good practice; it's an imperative. It ensures system stability, application performance, and fairness in multi-tenant scenarios. But it's not a set-and-forget affair. It requires continuous monitoring, understanding, and adjustment—a balancing act that, when executed well, ensures the harmonious coexistence of applications in the vibrant world of containers.

Chapter IX

Real-world Case Studies

Case Study 1:
Setting up a Continuous Integration pipeline with Docker

Continuous Integration (CI) has become integral to modern software development. The fundamental idea behind continuous integration (CI) is the regular merging of code changes into a common repository, which facilitates early problem discovery and guarantees quick software delivery. Docker, a pivotal tool in containerization, has gained immense traction for its ability to create consistent environments, leading to more reliable software delivery. The combination of CI and Docker has the potential to revolutionize development pipelines, creating a consistent and efficient workflow. This section delves into a case study of setting up a Continuous Integration pipeline using Docker, capturing the endeavor's steps, challenges, and outcomes.

Introduction to the Project:

Our subject for this case study is a mid-sized web application. The tech stack comprises of a Node.js backend, a React frontend, and a MongoDB database. The application development team has been experiencing inconsistencies in deployments. While the application might work seamlessly in a developer's local environment, it often breaks when deployed to production. The team hypothesized that the key to resolving these issues lay in implementing a robust CI process, and Docker was selected as the tool to achieve this uniformity.

Step 1: Dockerizing the Application:

Before introducing a CI pipeline, it was imperative to dockerize the application. Dockerfiles were created for both the frontend and the backend services. For the backend, a base image of node:alpine was chosen for its lightweight nature. The Dockerfile instructions encompassed setting up the working directory, copying package files, installing dependencies, copying source files, and finally, exposing the required port. Similarly, a Dockerfile was crafted for the frontend using a base React image and analogous steps.

An official MongoDB Docker image was employed to handle the MongoDB instance, eliminating the need for a custom Dockerfile. With individual Dockerfiles in place, a docker-compose.yml file was established to manage these services collectively, ensuring they could communicate seamlessly and replicate the production environment.

Step 2: Setting Up the CI Service:

For this case study, Jenkins was the CI server of choice due to its widespread use, extensive community support, and compatibility with Docker. Jenkins was set up on a virtual machine, and the necessary plugins for Docker and GitHub (the repository hosting service in use) were installed.

The application repository on GitHub was configured to send a webhook to Jenkins whenever there was a push to the repository. This triggered the CI process on Jenkins, defined as a Jenkins Pipeline.

Step 3: Defining the CI Pipeline:

The Jenkins Pipeline was crafted using a Jenkinsfile, a text file delineating the steps to be executed as part of the CI process. The steps were as follows:

Pull the Latest Code: Every time there was a push to the repository, Jenkins would pull the latest code.

Build Docker Images: Using the Dockerfiles present in the repository, Jenkins would build Docker images for the frontend, backend, and database.

Run Tests: With the images built, Docker containers were spun up using the docker-compose command. Automated tests, already written by the development team, were then executed within these containers. This ensured that the tests ran in an environment identical to production.

Feedback: If the tests passed, a success message was relayed to the team. Conversely, the team was immediately notified if any tests failed, ensuring rapid response and resolution.

Step 4: Iterations and Challenges:

The initial setup, though functional, was challenging. Some images took longer to build, making the process inefficient. To combat this, base images were occasionally switched to more lightweight versions, or pre-built images with common dependencies were used to speed up the process.

Another challenge encountered was network-related. Ensuring that the containers could communicate with each other, especially when tests involved multiple services, required tweaking the Docker Compose configurations and ensuring the correct ports were exposed and linked.

Step 5: Outcomes and Benefits:

After ironing out the initial challenges, the CI pipeline with Docker started showcasing its advantages. The consistency between development, testing, and production environments was the most significant improvement. Developers were confident that if their code passed tests in the CI pipeline, it would function correctly in production.

Besides consistency, the CI process fostered a culture of regular testing and feedback. The team became more proactive in addressing issues, leading to higher code quality and faster release cycles.

In conclusion, this case study underscores the transformative potential of integrating Docker with Continuous Integration. While the journey was interspersed with learning curves and challenges, software reliability, developer confidence, and delivery speed outcomes were noteworthy. The marriage of Docker's consistent environments with the regular feedback loops of CI created a synergistic effect, elevating the standards of software development and delivery. As organizations strive for rapid yet reliable software releases, tools and practices like these will undoubtedly be at the forefront, driving the evolution of modern development paradigms.

Case Study 2:
Microservices deployment with Docker Swarm

In the dynamic world of software architecture, microservices have emerged as a promising pattern, fragmenting monolithic applications into smaller, independent services. While microservices offer modularity, scalability, and easier management, deploying and orchestrating these services introduces challenges. Introducing Docker Swarm—a native clustering and orchestration tool for Docker, designed to manage a swarm of Docker nodes as a single virtual system. This section unveils a detailed case study of deploying a microservices-based application using Docker Swarm, mapping the journey from conceptualization to realization and the subsequent outcomes.

Introduction to the Project:

Our focal project is an e-commerce platform developed by a startup. The platform is divided into various microservices: User Management, Product Catalog, Order Processing, Payment, and Review and Ratings. Previously, the platform was a monolithic application. But as it grew, the team realized the advantages of breaking it down into microservices. However, managing deployments, scaling, and ensuring resilience for these microservices became paramount, leading to Docker Swarm's exploration and eventual adoption.

Step 1: Dockerizing the Microservices:

Before deploying with Docker Swarm, each microservice was containerized. Dockerfiles were curated for each service. The choice of base images was tailored according to the technology stack of the respective service. For instance, the Product Catalog, built with Python's Flask, utilized a lightweight Python base image. Each Dockerfile was meticulously crafted, incorporating best practices like minimizing layers and optimizing image size.

Step 2: Setting Up the Docker Swarm Cluster:

The heart of this endeavor was setting up the Docker Swarm cluster. Docker Swarm employs the manager-worker paradigm. A few nodes (servers) were designated as managers responsible for orchestrating the swarm, while the rest were worker nodes, executing the tasks.

The initialization of the swarm was performed on one of the servers, marking it as the leader manager. Other manager nodes and worker nodes subsequently joined this swarm. With the cluster in place, the team had a unified system where they could deploy and manage their microservices.

Step 3: Deploying Services with Stack Files:

Docker Swarm introduces the concept of stacks—a group of connected services that share dependencies and can be orchestrated as well as scaled together. For the e-commerce platform, a docker-compose.yml file, often referred to as the stack file in the context of Swarm, was authored. This file defined each microservice, its image, network configurations, dependencies, and other essential parameters.

Deployment was initiated using the docker stack deploy command, which took this stack file as an argument. Swarm's orchestrator ensured the services were distributed across nodes, keeping in mind the desired state and the current state of the cluster.

Step 4: Scaling and Load Balancing:

One of Docker Swarm's standout features is its ability to scale services seamlessly. The e-commerce platform witnessed high traffic on events like sales, requiring the Order Processing and Payment microservices to handle a higher load. With a simple docker service scale command, these services were scaled out, creating multiple replicas that were automatically distributed across the worker nodes.

Furthermore, Docker Swarm comes with an inbuilt load balancer. As services were scaled, Swarm's routing mesh ensured that incoming requests were evenly distributed among service replicas, optimizing resource utilization and ensuring high availability.

Step 5: Handling Failures and Ensuring Resilience:

No deployment strategy is complete without addressing failures. Docker Swarm constantly monitors the state of services. If a service fails or a node becomes unresponsive, Swarm detects this anomaly. It then reschedules the tasks of the failed service or node to healthy nodes, ensuring uninterrupted service.

For our e-commerce platform, this feature was invaluable. In one instance, during a peak sales period, a worker node experienced an outage. However, Swarm's automatic rescheduling ensured that the services running on that node were swiftly shifted to other available nodes, averting potential downtime.

Step 6: Challenges and Iterations:

While Docker Swarm offered many out-of-the-box solutions, the deployment journey had its challenges. One such challenge was stateful services, like databases. Microservices often rely on databases to retain state, and these databases need persistent storage. Docker containers, being ephemeral, posed a dilemma. The solution was to use Docker volumes, ensuring data persisted beyond the lifecycle of a container.

Another challenge was inter-service communication. As microservices often depend on one another, ensuring they can discover and communicate became crucial. The solution lay in Docker's inbuilt DNS server. Each service was given a unique DNS name, and services could use these names to discover and interact with each other.

In conclusion, deploying the e-commerce platform's microservices using Docker Swarm was a blend of strategic planning, execution, and iterative learning. The platform benefitted immensely, witnessing improved scalability, high availability, and efficient resource utilization.

This case study accentuates Docker Swarm's prowess in managing microservices deployments. By abstracting complexities and offering features like load balancing, automatic scaling, and failure recovery, Swarm enables organizations to focus on core development. As microservices continue to dominate the architectural landscape, tools like Docker Swarm will undoubtedly play a pivotal role in ensuring these services are deployed, managed, and scaled efficiently. The story of the e-commerce platform serves as a testament to Swarm's capabilities, offering insights and inspiration for organizations embarking on a similar journey.

Case Study 3: Database scaling and replication with Docker

In the digital era, databases lie at the heart of almost every application, storing vast information, from user profiles to transaction records. As applications grow, so does the load on these databases, necessitating efficient scaling and replication strategies. Docker, renowned for its containerization technology, can be an ally in this quest. This section offers a comprehensive insight into a case study where Docker was employed for database scaling and replication, shedding light on this endeavor's processes, challenges, and outcomes.

Introduction to the Project:

The subject of this case study is an online content platform, catering to millions of users daily. With an ever-growing user base and expanding content library, the platform's PostgreSQL database was under immense pressure. Queries were slowing down, and there was a looming risk of downtimes. The platform's technical team discerned two primary needs: horizontal scaling to distribute the load and replication to ensure data redundancy and availability. Docker emerged as the chosen tool to facilitate this.

Step 1: Containerizing the Database:

The journey commenced with containerizing the PostgreSQL database. Using the official PostgreSQL Docker image as the foundation, a Dockerfile was authored to customize configurations specific to the platform's needs. This containerized version ensured the database was isolated, consistent, and could be easily replicated across different environments.

Step 2: Setting Up Database Replication:

Replication ensures that data is duplicated across multiple locations, providing redundancy and increasing data availability. The platform opted for a Master-Slave replication setup.

Master Database: This was the primary database, catering to all write operations. Once containerized, configurations were tweaked to designate this PostgreSQL instance as the master.

Slave Databases: These databases were read-only replicas of the master database. Multiple slave instances were spun up using Docker, each with configurations indicating the master from which they should replicate data.

Using Docker's networking capabilities, a dedicated network was set up to ensure seamless communication between the master and slave databases.

Step 3: Horizontal Scaling with Database Sharding:

With replication in place, the next challenge was to distribute the database load. The platform decided to implement horizontal scaling through sharding. Instead of having one massive database, the data was partitioned into smaller, faster, more easily managed databases called shards.

Docker played a pivotal role here. Each shard, essentially a separate PostgreSQL instance, was containerized. Docker Compose managed these multiple containers, ensuring they were interconnected and ran harmoniously.

Based on content IDs, a sharding key determined how data was distributed among these shards. When a query arrived, the application logic, armed with this sharding key, knew precisely which Docker container (or shard) to communicate with, optimizing query times.

Step 4: Ensuring Data Consistency:

A significant challenge in database replication and sharding is ensuring data consistency. The platform had to ascertain that all slave databases were synchronized with the master and that shards remained consistent with their data distribution.

Docker's orchestration capabilities, combined with PostgreSQL's native replication mechanisms, were crucial here. Regular health checks were instituted, and any anomalies in replication lag or shard distributions triggered alerts, allowing the team to intervene and rectify.

Step 5: Performance Tuning and Load Balancing:

Merely setting up replication and sharding wasn't the endgame. The team used Docker's resource management capabilities, like setting

CPU and memory limits, to optimize each database container's performance.

Moreover, a load balancer was introduced. Write requests were routed directly to the master database, but read requests were distributed among the slave databases, ensuring balanced loads and rapid query resolutions.

Step 6: Challenges and Overcoming Them:
While Docker streamlined many aspects of this endeavor, challenges were inevitable. One prominent issue was persistent storage. Docker containers are inherently ephemeral, so ensuring data persisted beyond the container's lifecycle was vital. Docker volumes were the solution, allowing data to be stored outside the container, ensuring its longevity.

Another challenge was the initial data migration to this new setup. With live users, ensuring zero downtime and data consistency during this transition was arduous. The team employed a phased approach, gradually redirecting traffic to the new setup while constantly monitoring for discrepancies.

In conclusion, this case study encapsulates the transformative journey of an online content platform as it grappled with and overcame database scaling and replication challenges using Docker. The result was a robust, scalable, and resilient database system, ensuring fast query resolutions, high availability, and data redundancy.

Docker's capabilities, ranging from easy replication to resource optimization, were instrumental in this transformation. However, it wasn't just about the technology, but also the vision, strategy, and meticulous execution of the platform's technical team.

As organizations scale and their data needs amplify, this case study serves as both an inspiration and a roadmap. It underscores the importance of proactive scaling and the pivotal role tools like Docker can play in ensuring databases remain the robust backbone of applications, even in the face of escalating demands.

Chapter X

Best Practices and Tips

Efficient image building

Docker images are the bedrock upon which the entire system functions in containerization. These images, essentially file system snapshots, serve as the blueprint from which containers are instantiated. Given their foundational role, how these images are constructed significantly impacts performance, security, and efficiency. A poorly crafted image can result in bloated containers, longer deployment times, security vulnerabilities, and unnecessary overhead. As such, efficient image building isn't just a technical nicety; it's an operational imperative.

To comprehend the essence of efficient image building, one must first understand the layered architecture of Docker images. Every command in a Dockerfile, the script that defines how an image is built, creates a new layer. These layers are stacked atop each other, forming the final image. The layered approach offers numerous benefits, including caching, reuse, and incremental updates. However, if not utilized judiciously, it can lead to inefficiencies and bloat.

One of the foundational principles of efficient image building is minimizing the number of layers. While this may seem counterintuitive given Docker's layered architecture, the rationale is rooted in efficiency. Each layer adds overhead, both in terms of storage and runtime performance. By combining commands in the Dockerfile and being informed about the order of commands, developers can reduce the number of layers, leading to leaner images. For instance, instead of having separate RUN commands for installing packages, they can be combined into a single command, reducing layers and making better use of cachi

Caching is another cornerstone of efficient image building. Docker caches layers, meaning that if no changes are detected since the last build, it will reuse the existing layer rather than recreate it. This speeds up image building considerably. However, to use caching effectively, one must be strategic about the order of Dockerfile commands. Commands that change frequently should be placed later in the Dockerfile, ensuring that more stable layers are cached and reused, minimizing the build time.

Yet, efficiency isn't solely about speed; it's also about size. A bloated image, even if built quickly, can be detrimental regarding storage costs, transfer times, and container startup performance. Here, the choice of the base image plays a pivotal role. Many official images available on Docker Hub come in "slim" or "alpine" variants. These lightweight versions strip out unnecessary components, leading to smaller image sizes. By choosing such base images, developers can start with a minimal footprint, adding only what's necessary for their application.

In pursuing minimalism, another best practice involves cleaning up within the same layer where changes are made. For instance, it's prudent to remove the package cache within the same RUN command if installing packages. This ensures that the intermediate bloat introduced during installation doesn't reach the final image layer.

Security, while not always directly associated with efficiency, plays a crucial role in image building. An efficient image is also one free from vulnerabilities. Regularly updating the base image and installed packages ensures that known vulnerabilities are patched. Additionally, tools like Docker's scan command or third-party solutions can be used to scan images for vulnerabilities, ensuring that images are efficient and secure.

Beyond these principles, developers should be aware of specific anti-patterns. Avoiding the use of the latest tag ensures that builds are predictable and reproducible. Relying on the latest tag can lead to unexpected changes, as this tag can point to different actual versions over time. Also, embedding sensitive information like secrets or credentials directly into the image is a grave mistake. Not only does this present a security risk, but it also ties the image to specific environments or configurations, reducing its portability and reusability.

In conclusion, the art and science of building efficient Docker images are a confluence of strategic layer management, judicious command ordering, base image selection, and a relentless focus on minimalism and security. It's a discipline that requires both foresight and understanding of the intricate dance of dependencies and commands that go into constructing an image. When executed well, the result is a lightweight, fast, secure, and optimal Docker image that is a solid foundation for applications in a containerized world. As containerization continues to permeate modern software delivery, the significance of efficient image building will only amplify, making it an indispensable skill for developers and operations teams alike.

Monitoring and logging containers

The surge in containerization, spearheaded by technologies like Docker, has redefined the paradigms of application deployment and scaling. Containers, with their promise of isolation, portability, and reproducibility, have become the preferred vehicle for deploying microservices and cloud-native applications. However, with this adoption comes a new set of challenges: monitoring and logging these ephemeral, dynamically orchestrated environments. While containers have revolutionized deployment, they've also introduced complexities in understanding application health, performance, and behavior. As such, adept monitoring and logging have emerged as crucial for maintaining containerized applications' stability, security, and efficiency.

At a foundational level, monitoring in containerized environments is about understanding the state and performance of individual containers and the applications running within them. Unlike traditional monolithic applications where performance bottlenecks or failures might be easier to trace, containerized applications often involve multiple interacting containers, possibly spread across different hosts or data centers. This distributed and dynamic nature necessitates a more nuanced approach to monitoring.

Traditional system-level metrics like CPU usage, memory consumption, disk I/O, and network bandwidth remain vital in a containerized world. These metrics provide insights into the resource usage and performance of containers. However, they are just the tip of the iceberg. A single host might run multiple containers, and a single application might span multiple containers, so container-specific metrics are needed. These might include the container creation and termination rate, the number of running containers, container health statuses, and more. Such metrics offer a granular view of the container landscape, highlighting potential issues like resource contention, container churn, or service disruptions.

But monitoring isn't solely about collecting metrics; it's also about setting meaningful alerts based on these metrics. In dynamic environments, thresholds can be fluid, and what constitutes "normal" can vary. Adaptive alerting mechanisms that factor in historical data, patterns, and machine learning can be invaluable. These systems can recognize anomalies, predict potential issues, and trigger alerts or even automated actions to mitigate problems.

Parallel to monitoring stands the equally vital discipline of logging. Logs offer a ground-level, detailed narrative of events if monitoring provides a bird's-eye view of the system's state. Logs become the primary source of truth in containerized environments when diagnosing issues, understanding application behavior, or tracing transactions across services.

However, logging in containerized setups comes with its set of challenges. Given the transient nature of containers—where containers can be created and destroyed on-demand—the traditional model of storing logs locally on the host becomes untenable. If a container is terminated, its logs would be lost unless persisted elsewhere. As a result, centralized logging solutions have become the norm. Tools and platforms like the ELK Stack (Elasticsearch, Logstash, Kibana), Fluentd, and Graylog, among others, provide mechanisms to aggregate logs from multiple containers, store them efficiently, and offer querying and visualization capabilities.

Beyond centralization, log enrichment becomes crucial in containerized setups. Since logs might originate from various services and containers, adding metadata—like the container ID, service name, host information, and more—can provide context to the logs. Such enrichment aids in correlating logs, tracing requests, and diagnosing issues.

Security is another dimension of logging that must be considered. Logs often contain sensitive information, be it user data, system details, or potential vulnerabilities. Ensuring that logs are transmitted securely, stored encrypted, and accessed only by authorized personnel is paramount. Additionally, given regulatory landscapes like GDPR, CCPA, and others, ensuring logs don't inadvertently store personally identifiable information, or PII, becomes essential.

In conclusion, as containerization continues to shape the contours of modern software deployment, the twin pillars of monitoring and logging stand as essential guardians of system health, security, and efficiency. They provide the visibility and insights necessary to navigate the complexities of dynamic, distributed environments. Yet, their implementation demands a blend of technical acumen, strategic thinking, and an understanding of the ever-evolving landscape of tools and best practices. When orchestrated well, monitoring and logging mitigate risks and drive optimizations, fostering a culture of continuous improvement in the vibrant world of containerized applications.

Ensuring container health

In the grand tapestry of modern software infrastructures, containers have emerged as quintessential elements, encapsulating applications and their dependencies into standardized units for development, shipment, and deployment. The sheer brilliance of containers lies in their portability and consistency, ensuring that what works on a developer's machine also runs seamlessly in production. Yet, as with any component in software engineering, containers are not impervious to issues. Ensuring their health, therefore, becomes paramount in the quest for stable, scalable, and efficient software delivery.

Container health is multifaceted. It encompasses the container's operational state and the application running within, its resource usage, network connectivity, and its interactions with other containers or services. Just like a physician wouldn't merely check a patient's heartbeat but would consider a gamut of vital signs and other indicators, ensuring container health demands a holistic approach.

One might wonder why container health is of such significance. The reason is two-fold. First, containers play a pivotal role in architectures especially designed around microservices. A single failing container can cascade into system-wide disruptions, especially if it's a critical service. Second, there's an inherent unpredictability given the dynamic nature of container orchestration platforms like Kubernetes or Docker Swarm, where containers might be frequently created, moved, or destroyed. Given changing workloads, network conditions, or interactions, a healthy container might encounter issues moments later.

Understanding this, the first line of defense in ensuring container health is monitoring. Continuous and granular monitoring of containers provides real-time insights into their state. Traditional metrics like CPU usage, memory consumption, disk I/O, and network throughput are essential. Still, in the container world, additional metrics like container start/stop rates, the number of active containers, or container-specific error rates exist. Tools like Prometheus, cAdvisor, or Datadog, among others, can provide these insights, helping operators and developers identify issues before they escalate.

Yet, merely collecting metrics is half the battle. Actively probing container health is the next step. This is where health checks come into play. Health checks are periodic tests against a container to ensure it operates as expected. These can be as simple as checking if a container is responsive, like sending an HTTP request to a web server container, or more complex, verifying if a database container can read/write data. Platforms like Docker and Kubernetes offer native mechanisms to define and run health checks, ensuring that containers start successfully and continue functioning as intended throughout their lifecycle.

However, even with rigorous monitoring and health checks, issues can arise. In such scenarios, automated recovery mechanisms become invaluable. Consider a container running out of memory due to a sudden surge in user requests. Instead of crashing, orchestration platforms can be configured to automatically restart the container or even spawn additional containers to share the load. This resilience, baked into the system's design, ensures that transient issues don't translate into prolonged outages or degraded user experiences.

Beyond these technical mechanisms, ensuring container health also involves best practices in container design and deployment. Containers should be designed to be stateless, where possible, ensuring that they can be destroyed or replicated without adverse effects. Adhering to the principle of single responsibility, where a container does one thing and does it well, can mitigate complexities. Regularly updating containers and keeping them patched against known vulnerabilities, ensures they remain secure against potential threats.

Yet, even as organizations put in place these mechanisms, human vigilance remains irreplaceable. Cultivating a culture of observability, where developers and operators are attuned to system behavior, often preemptively recognizing patterns or anomalies, adds another layer of assurance. Collaborative platforms that amalgamate logs, metrics, and traces, providing a unified view of the system, aid in this endeavor.

In conclusion, in their ephemeral and dynamic glory, containers have redefined the paradigms of software deployment and scaling. Yet, their vitality is contingent on their health. Ensuring container health, therefore, is not a mere operational necessity but a strategic imperative. It weaves together the threads of monitoring, proactive testing, automated recovery, best practices, and human vigilance into a cohesive tapestry, safeguarding the very heartbeats of modern software infrastructures. As containers continue their march, shaping the horizons of cloud-native landscapes, nurturing their health will remain central to the narratives of reliability, performance, and excellence.

Chapter XI

Advanced Docker Concepts

Multi-stage builds

Multi-stage builds in Docker have emerged as a powerful technique to streamline the containerization process, reduce image size, and enhance the overall efficiency of building and deploying applications. Docker, a popular containerization platform, allows developers to package applications along with their dependencies into lightweight, portable containers. However, container images can quickly become bloated with unnecessary files and dependencies, leading to longer build times and larger image sizes. Multi-stage builds address this issue by enabling developers to create optimized Docker images through a sequence of build stages, resulting in leaner and more efficient containers.

The concept of multi-stage builds was introduced in Docker 17.05, and it has since gained widespread adoption in the containerization ecosystem. This approach involves defining multiple stages within a Dockerfile, each with its own set of instructions and a separate base image. Each stage serves a specific purpose in the build process, such as compiling source code, installing dependencies, or generating artifacts. The final image is derived from the last stage and contains only the necessary files and libraries to run the application, eliminating extraneous baggage.

One of the primary advantages of multi-stage builds is the significant reduction in image size. In traditional Docker builds, intermediate layers accumulate in the image, resulting in larger file sizes. These images can be cumbersome to transfer across networks and consume more storage space. Multi-stage builds address this problem by discarding unnecessary files and dependencies in each intermediate stage. As a result, the final image contains only what is essential for running the application, resulting in a much smaller footprint.

Another notable benefit of multi-stage builds is improved build speed. In a monolithic Dockerfile, all build steps are executed sequentially, even if some are unrelated to the final application. This can be time-consuming, mainly when dealing with complex applications with multiple dependencies. With multi-stage builds, each stage is isolated and can be executed in parallel, making the build process more efficient. Developers can also use caching at each stage, preventing redundant work when the source code or dependencies have not changed.

Maintaining security is crucial in containerization, and multi-stage builds contribute to this by reducing the attack surface. Traditional Docker images may include unnecessary development tools, libraries, or system binaries, potentially exposing vulnerabilities. Multi-stage builds eliminate these extraneous components from the final image, making it more secure. Moreover, by discarding intermediate stages, sensitive information, such as API keys or database credentials, can be effectively protected during the build process.

Multi-stage builds are particularly valuable when applications must be built from source code or require multiple build steps. Consider a web application that relies on various libraries and dependencies during development but only needs the compiled application code and runtime dependencies in the final image. By leveraging multi-stage builds, developers can separate the development and runtime environments, resulting in a cleaner, more efficient container.

Docker's support for multi-stage builds also extends to flexibility in choosing base images for each stage. This allows developers to tailor each stage to their specific requirements. For instance, one stage may use a lightweight base image optimized for compiling code, while another may use a smaller image tailored for running the application. This flexibility enables developers to balance image size and functionality, ensuring that the final container meets both performance and resource constraints.

While multi-stage builds offer numerous benefits, they also come with some considerations and best practices. First, it's essential to plan and organize the build stages effectively. Each stage should have a clear purpose, and dependencies should be installed and configured correctly to ensure a successful build. Additionally, developers should be mindful of the order in which stages are defined, as later stages can copy artifacts from earlier ones.

Caching is another crucial aspect of optimizing multi-stage builds. Docker can cache intermediate stages based on changes in the source code or dependencies. Developers should structure their Dockerfiles to take advantage of caching whenever possible, as this can significantly reduce build times. However, it's essential to be cautious when using caching for stages that involve sensitive data, as cached data can persist in layers.

Furthermore, monitoring and maintaining multi-stage Dockerfiles can become complex as the number of stages increases. Developers should document the purpose of each step and keep Dockerfiles well-organized to ensure easy maintenance and collaboration among team members.

In conclusion, multi-stage builds in Docker have revolutionized the containerization process by addressing issues related to image size, build speed, security, and flexibility. By breaking down the build process into distinct stages, developers can create leaner, more efficient container images that contain only what is necessary to run the application. This approach is particularly valuable when applications require multiple build steps or have complex dependencies. While multi-stage builds offer numerous advantages, they require careful planning, consideration of caching strategies, and effective documentation to maximize their benefits. Overall, multi-stage builds have become a fundamental technique in the Docker ecosystem, empowering developers to create optimized containers that enhance the deployment and scalability of their applications.

Optimizing Docker for production

Since its inception, Docker has become an indispensable tool in the software development world. Its promise to encapsulate applications with all their dependencies into lightweight containers has revolutionized how software is packaged, distributed, and run. While Docker shines in development environments due to its consistency and portability, the challenge often arises when transitioning to a production setting. As with any technology, Docker's true prowess is realized when it's finely tuned for a production environment. This entails ensuring that containers are functional, secure, scalable, and performance-oriented.

One of the foremost concerns when moving Docker to production is security. Containers, by nature, share the host's kernel, making them lighter than traditional VMs. However, this also introduces potential vulnerabilities if not properly managed. The first step in securing Docker is to ensure that the Docker daemon, which runs with root privileges, is protected. Binding the Docker daemon to a Unix socket rather than a TCP port, ensuring encrypted communication, and employing user namespaces to map root inside the container to a non-root user outside are pivotal to safeguarding the daemon.

Images form the foundation of containers; hence, their integrity is paramount. Always source images from trusted repositories or build your own from verified and secure base images. Regularly scanning images for vulnerabilities using tools like Clair or Trivy helps keep potential security threats at bay.

Network security is equally critical. Docker provides network modes like bridge, host, and overlay, each with its implications. By default, containers can communicate freely, which may not always be desired in production. Employing user-defined bridge networks or leveraging Docker Swarm's encrypted overlay networks can offer isolation and security.

With security foundations in place, the focus shifts to performance. At its core, Docker relies on namespaces and cgroups for container isolation and resource allocation. By fine-tuning these configurations, one can ensure optimal performance. Setting resource limits, such as CPU and memory constraints, prevents any single container from monopolizing system resources. This is especially crucial in a microservices architecture where multiple services run concurrently.

Often overlooked, storage plays a pivotal role in Docker's performance. Docker provides various storage drivers, each optimized for specific use cases. Overlay2, for instance, is recommended by Docker due to its balance of performance and stability. However, it's crucial to monitor I/O performance and ensure that the underlying file system is conducive to the chosen storage driver.

Docker's architecture makes it inherently scalable. However, manually managing a large number of containers quickly becomes cumbersome. This is where orchestration tools like Docker Swarm or Kubernetes come into play. They handle the deployment and scaling of containers and manage networking, storage, and load balancing. In a production environment, where uptime and resilience are critical, these orchestrators can detect and respond to container failures, ensuring that applications remain available.

Load balancing, a key scalability component, ensures that incoming requests are evenly distributed across containers. Tools like Docker's built-in load balancer or external solutions like HAProxy or Traefik can be employed depending on the complexity and the scale of the application.

No production system is complete without robust monitoring and logging solutions. Monitoring provides insights into container health, resource usage, and performance bottlenecks. Integrating monitoring solutions like Prometheus with visualization tools like Grafana can offer real-time metrics and dashboards. Logging, on the other hand, aids in troubleshooting and auditing. Centralized logging solutions, such as the ELK stack (Elasticsearch, Logstash, Kibana), can aggregate logs from all containers, providing a unified view.

Continuous integration and continuous deployment pipelines further augment Docker's production readiness. Automated testing and deployment processes ensure that containers are always in their desired state, free from manual errors. Tools like Jenkins or GitLab CI can be integrated with Docker to automate these pipelines, ensuring that only validated and tested containers reach the production environment.

Transitioning Docker from a development tool to a production-ready platform requires a holistic approach that melds security, performance, scalability, and maintainability. By securing the foundational elements like the Docker daemon, images, and networks, we lay the groundwork for a robust environment. Performance tuning ensures that applications run efficiently, while scalability provisions cater to growing demands. Monitoring and maintainability round off the optimization process, ensuring that Docker runs flawlessly and remains agile to changing needs.

In a production context, Docker represents more than just containerization; it embodies a shift towards a more modular, scalable, and resilient software infrastructure. With the proper optimizations, Docker can power the most demanding production environments, reflecting its true potential in reshaping the software landscape. As we rush towards an increasingly digital future, technologies like Docker will stand at the forefront, driving innovation and setting new standards for software deployment and management.

Docker plugins and extensions

In the modern technology landscape, Docker has emerged as a pivotal tool, allowing developers and system administrators to package, distribute, and manage applications within containers. These containers encapsulate an application and all its dependencies in an established unit for software development. However, as with any technology, specific needs and use cases always go beyond the core functionality. This is where Docker plugins and extensions come into play, extending Docker's capabilities and ensuring it remains a flexible tool for a diverse array of tasks. This section delves deep into Docker plugins and extensions, discussing their nature, importance, and how they enhance Docker's core experience.

To begin with, it is essential to understand what Docker plugins and extensions are. Docker plugins are out-of-process extensions that integrate seamlessly with the Docker engine, adding new functionalities not available in the core Docker platform. They provide extended networking, storage, and logging capabilities, among other aspects. For example, while Docker has its default storage drivers, a storage plugin might allow users to integrate with other solutions that suit their needs, such as distributed storage systems or unique filesystems. Similarly, network plugins might allow for connections with specialized networking equipment or software-defined networks, enhancing Docker's networking capabilities.

The architecture of Docker inherently supports plugins. When a Docker engine requires a specific functionality, it consults with the relevant plugin, effectively allowing third-party solutions to act as if they were part of Docker's core. This modular approach ensures that Docker remains lightweight, as users can choose to install only the plugins relevant to their needs, avoiding unnecessary bloat.

Extensions generally refer to tools or additional software that work alongside Docker to provide supplementary functionalities. These could range from CI/CD tools that integrate with Docker for streamlined deployment processes to monitoring and logging solutions that help keep track of containerized applications' performance and health. Extensions, while not directly modifying

Docker's core capabilities, work with it, creating a more holistic solution for developers and administrators.

The significance of plugins and extensions cannot be understated. At its core, Docker is designed to be a general-purpose containerization tool. However, every enterprise or individual might have specific requirements that don't align perfectly with Docker's out-of-the-box capabilities. By allowing for plugins and extensions, Docker acknowledges the diverse ecosystem it operates within. Instead of attempting to be a monolithic solution that caters to every possible need – which could lead to complexity and inefficiency – Docker focuses on doing what it does best, while enabling third parties to contribute functionalities that address niche requirements.

Furthermore, the existence of plugins and extensions fosters a community-driven approach. Open-source contributors, third-party vendors, and enterprises can develop their plugins or extensions tailored to specific needs, leading to a richer ecosystem where innovation thrives. As various industry players encounter unique challenges, they can develop solutions through plugins and extensions, which can then be shared with the extensive community. This ensures that Docker remains adaptable to evolving technology landscapes and industry needs.

However, with the advantages come specific challenges. Given the open nature of plugins and extensions, there might be concerns related to security, maintenance, and compatibility. Users must exercise due diligence when integrating third-party solutions, ensuring they come from reputable sources, are well-maintained, and are compatible with their specific Docker versions. Thankfully, Docker has recognized these challenges and offers a managed plugin system, where plugins are packaged, versioned, and distributed in a standardized manner, somewhat mitigating these concerns.

In conclusion, Docker plugins and extensions are crucial in enhancing and customizing the Docker experience. They acknowledge a diverse and ever-evolving technological landscape, ensuring that Docker remains relevant, adaptable, and powerful. While they come with their set of challenges, their benefits – in terms of flexibility, community-driven innovation, and specialized functionalities – are undeniable. As Docker continues to dominate the containerization space, plugins and extensions will undeniably remain integral to its success, ensuring it meets the diverse needs of its global user base.

Chapter XII

The Future of
Docker and Containerization

Emerging technologies in the container space

The modern software landscape has witnessed a significant evolution over the past few years, and containers have been at the forefront of this change. Containers provide a consistent environment to run applications by packaging the application and its dependencies together. While Docker paved the way for widespread container adoption, the container ecosystem is vast and rapidly evolving. This section delves into the emerging technologies in the container space, highlighting innovations and their impacts on software development, deployment, and operation.

When discussing the container space, it is impossible not to mention Kubernetes. Initially created by Google and later donated to the Cloud Native Computing Foundation (or CNCF), Kubernetes, an open-source container orchestration platform, has experienced an explosive growth. While Kubernetes itself isn't new, many emerging technologies and tools build upon or integrate with it, aiming to enhance its capabilities or streamline its complexities. From automated scaling to self-healing and rolling updates, Kubernetes has become the de facto norm for managing large-scale containerized applications. However, the rise of Kubernetes has also brought forth a need for tools and platforms that address its inherent complexities.

One such emerging area is "Service Mesh." Service mesh technologies, like Istio and Linkerd, have gained traction as microservices architectures become more common. Microservices often involve complex communication patterns, and a service mesh provides a dedicated infrastructure layer to handle service-to-service communication, making it more observable, manageable, and secure. With a service mesh, developers can implement functionalities like traffic routing, load balancing, and failure recovery without modifying the application code. Moreover, it provides insights into the communication between services, aiding in monitoring and troubleshooting.

Another significant area of innovation in the container ecosystem is "Serverless" or Function-as-a-Service (FaaS) platforms. Tools like Knative, which builds upon Kubernetes, aim to provide serverless capabilities in containerized environments. These platforms allow developers to focus solely on writing code, without worrying on the underlying infrastructure. The infrastructure dynamically allocates resources, scales in real-time based on demand, and the developers are billed only for the actual compute time their code consumes. Combining serverless paradigms with containers means that developers get the best of both worlds - the consistency and portability of containers and the convenience and efficiency of serverless.

Security in the container space has also seen many emerging solutions, given the unique challenges posed by containerized environments. Traditional security tools and approaches might not be well-suited for dynamic, ephemeral container environments. New solutions like Falco, an open-source cloud-native runtime security project, aim to detect malicious activity in real-time, providing deep insights into the behavior of containers. Such tools use policy-driven approaches to ensure that any abnormal behavior within containers is promptly detected and addressed.

Storage solutions tailored for containerized environments represent another exciting area of development. Since containers are stateless and ephemeral, managing persistent data storage can be challenging. Emerging projects like Rook aim to turn distributed storage systems into self-managing, self-scaling, and self-healing storage services. Integrating directly with Kubernetes, Rook provides a cloud-native way to manage storage, ensuring data persistence and reliability in containerized deployments.

The container space's network aspect also sees innovative solutions. While containers have their isolated environments, they need to communicate – with each other, external services, and end-users. Technologies like Cilium, which provide API-aware network security, visibility, and load balancing, enhance how network operations are handled in containerized setups. These tools provide more granular control, security, and observability by understanding API or request level information.

The rise of edge computing has further influenced the container space. With the Internet of Things (IoT) devices proliferation and the need for low-latency applications, computing is moving closer to data sources, i.e., the 'edge.' Emerging projects like K3s, a lightweight Kubernetes distribution, are designed explicitly for edge and resource-constrained environments. By ensuring that container orchestration remains efficient, even in edge environments, these technologies are paving the way for a more distributed computing future.

Moreover, the sheer growth and adoption of containers have led to the emergence of specialized container platforms targeting specific industries or use cases. The container ecosystem's diversity is expanding from platforms tailored for data science workloads, ensuring a seamless transition from development to production for ML models, to solutions focusing on real-time, high-performance computing tasks.

In conclusion, while containers were a revolutionary concept when first introduced, the continuous evolution and innovation in the container space is nothing short of remarkable. The current trends indicate a focus on simplifying complexities, enhancing security, providing more granular control, and ensuring that containers are suited for diverse, modern computing needs, from cloud to edge. As these emerging technologies mature and new ones arise, the container space will undoubtedly remain a dynamic and exciting field, continuing to shape the future of software development and operations.

Integration with Kubernetes

In today's technology-driven landscape, Kubernetes has emerged as a centerpiece in container orchestration. Born out of Google's expertise with scaling applications, and afterwards donated to the Cloud Native Computing Foundation (or CNCF), Kubernetes has grown into a widely adopted platform that manages and orchestrates containerized applications. As organizations have embarked on their digital transformation journeys, integrating with Kubernetes has become paramount. This section delves deep into the intricacies of such integration, exploring the various facets, challenges, and transformative potential of aligning with Kubernetes.

At its heart, Kubernetes is designed to automate, deploy, scale, and operate application containers. Its dominance in the container orchestration sphere arises from its ability to abstract the infrastructure layer, allowing developers and operators to interact with clusters rather than individual machines. When one speaks of integration with Kubernetes, it covers a broad spectrum: from applications being adapted for deployment on Kubernetes, tools that enhance or complement its capabilities, to platforms being tailored to provide specialized Kubernetes experiences.

Starting with the application perspective, integration often begins with "containerization." Applications, especially legacy ones, might not be initially designed for container environments. The process involves encapsulating the application in a container with all its dependencies. Tools like Docker play a crucial role here, and once containerized, Kubernetes can manage applications. However, this is only the tip of the iceberg. True integration means understanding and leveraging Kubernetes-native features. This could involve adapting the application architecture to fit the microservices paradigm, designing for statelessness (or managing state effectively), and adopting Kubernetes primitives like Pods, Deployments, and Services for application management.

Beyond the application itself, integration extends to the entire DevOps lifecycle. Continuous Integration and Continuous Deployment pipelines, traditionally designed for monolithic application deployments, need rethinking. Emerging Kubernetes ecosystem tools like Jenkins X or Tekton have surfaced to address this, offering Kubernetes-native CI/CD experiences. These tools understand Kubernetes' nuances, providing seamless integration from code commit to deployment, respecting the dynamic nature of container orchestration.

Monitoring and logging represent another critical area of integration. Traditional monitoring solutions might not be well-suited for containerized environments' transient and dynamic nature. New-age tools like Prometheus (for monitoring) and Loki (for logging), which are built with Kubernetes in mind, offer deeper insights into cluster health, application performance, and logs in a Kubernetes-native way. Integration with such tools ensures that organizations can maintain the visibility and observability standards they are accustomed to, even in a Kubernetes-centric environment.

Security is a non-negotiable aspect, and integrating security solutions with Kubernetes is paramount. Given that Kubernetes has its own security challenges, tools like Aqua Security and Falco have emerged, providing runtime security for Kubernetes environments. These tools monitor the behavior of containers, ensuring compliance with set policies, and offering real-time threat detection. Integrating security tools with Kubernetes ensures that application workloads are safe and that the Kubernetes infrastructure itself is shielded from potential threats.

Networking in Kubernetes, with its own set of primitives like Services, Ingress, and Network Policies, requires a fresh approach. Integration with Kubernetes means understanding and adopting these primitives and potentially leveraging solutions like Calico or Cilium to enhance networking capabilities. These tools provide advanced networking features, from network segmentation to API-aware network security, ensuring that container communication remains seamless, scalable, and secure.

Storage, a cornerstone of many applications, poses challenges in Kubernetes, given its stateless design principle. Persistent storage solutions need to be integrated to ensure data durability and availability. Tools like Rook have emerged to bridge this gap, turning distributed storage systems into self-managing, self-scaling, and self-healing storage services while natively integrating with Kubernetes.

In the realm of user experience, Kubernetes, with its vast array of configurations and primitives, can be daunting. Hence, platforms like OpenShift by Red Hat have risen to the occasion, offering a tailored Kubernetes experience. They integrate developer tools, enhance default Kubernetes security, and offer a streamlined experience, making Kubernetes more accessible to a broader audience.

Challenges in Kubernetes integration are undeniable. The rapid evolution of the Kubernetes ecosystem means that tools and best practices are continuously evolving. Integrating with such a dynamic platform requires organizations to be agile, adaptable, and always in the learning mode. Legacy applications might need significant refactoring, and teams may need upskilling to harness the power of Kubernetes truly.

In conclusion, integration with Kubernetes is a multifaceted journey. The process is transformative, from adapting applications to incorporating tools that complement Kubernetes' capabilities. Kubernetes offers a promise – that of scalability, resilience, and agility. However, genuinely realizing this promise requires deep integration, understanding the platform's nuances, and aligning with its principles. As Kubernetes continues its march towards becoming the universal orchestration platform, the importance of effective integration only becomes more pronounced, heralding a new era of cloud-native applications and infrastructure.

Docker's role in serverless architecture

In the tapestry of modern software development, serverless architecture has emerged as a compelling paradigm, promising developers to focus solely on their code, while the underlying infrastructure, scaling, and operations are abstracted away. At the heart of this transformation is containerization, and Docker, a pioneering force in this domain, plays a pivotal role. This section delves deep into understanding Docker's position and influence within serverless architecture, the nuanced interplay of containers and serverless paradigms, and how Docker's evolution has shaped, and been shaped by, the serverless movement.

Since its inception, Docker has revolutionized how applications are packaged, distributed, and run. By providing a consistent environment through containers, Docker eliminated the age-old problem of "it works on my machine." In essence, Docker containers encapsulate an application and its dependencies in a unified package, ensuring that the application runs uniformly, irrespective of where the container is executed. This consistent environment, lightweight nature, and isolation capabilities make Docker containers an ideal candidate for the serverless world.

Serverless architecture, often epitomized by the Function-as-a-Service (FaaS) model, is all about executing application logic in response to events without maintaining a persistent server infrastructure. Under the hood, serverless platforms must rapidly start, run, and terminate instances of the application logic, often with varying workloads. Herein lies Docker's first significant contribution: rapid instantiation. Docker containers are lightweight and start quickly, aligning with serverless workloads' transient and dynamic nature. As serverless platforms handle incoming events, they can swiftly instantiate Docker containers to process them, ensuring low latency and efficient resource utilization.

However, Docker's influence in serverless architecture is not merely confined to its containerization capabilities. The Docker image, a static snapshot containing the application and its runtime, provides a standardized deployment unit. This standardization has profound implications in the serverless world. When developers write serverless functions, they must specify the runtime environment, dependencies, and configurations. Docker images, being a self-contained package, can be seamlessly used by serverless platforms as the unit of execution. Thus, developers can craft a Docker image containing their serverless function, and the serverless platform can execute it directly, leveraging Docker's consistency and isolation.

The serverless paradigm's modularity, where applications are broken down into individual functions or logic units, dovetails perfectly with Docker's microservices-driven approach. Docker has always championed the idea of breaking applications into smaller, manageable, and independent containers, mirroring the philosophy of serverless architectures. As organizations transitioned to microservices, Docker provided the tools and best practices to manage these services efficiently. When serverless emerged as a logical progression from microservices, Docker's existing tooling, practices, and community expertise provided a robust foundation to build upon.

Docker's ecosystem and tooling also play an instrumental role in the serverless arena. Docker Compose, for instance, allows developers to define and run multi-container applications. In a serverless context, where applications are composed of multiple independent functions, tools like Docker Compose can aid in locally developing, testing, and simulating serverless workflows, ensuring that the functions interact as expected.

However, it's essential to recognize the challenges and critiques as well. One of the critiques has been the cold start times, mainly when Docker containers are used in a serverless context. While containers are lightweight compared to virtual machines, there's still an overhead when initializing a new container, especially if the container image is large or if the application has extensive dependencies. Serverless platforms strive for minimal latency, and any delay in processing can harm the user experience. Thus, there's been a push towards optimizing Docker containers for serverless, ensuring they are minimal, optimized, and tailored for quick startups.

In the evolutionary journey of Docker and serverless, we've also seen symbiotic growth. As serverless architectures gained traction, there was a need for serverless platforms that could be run on-premises or in hybrid environments, not just on cloud providers. Solutions like OpenFaaS emerged, allowing organizations to build serverless functions using Docker containers, thereby combining the power of Docker's containerization with the flexibility of serverless architectures. Such platforms have democratized serverless, ensuring that it's not just confined to large cloud providers but accessible to organizations with varying infrastructure setups.

In conclusion, Docker's role in serverless architecture is multifaceted and profound. From providing the fundamental building block in the form of containers to influencing the very design and modularity of serverless applications, Docker has been both a catalyst and beneficiary of the serverless movement. The interplay between Docker and serverless is a testament to the adaptive and innovative nature of the software industry, where tools and paradigms coevolve, drawing from each other's strengths, addressing challenges, and collectively pushing the boundaries of what's possible in software development and deployment.

Conclusion

Summing up the Docker journey

As we near the end of this e-book, we must take a few moments to stand back, pause, and reflect on the life-changing experience that we have been on, thanks to Docker. Over the past few years, container technology has significantly expanded the range of capabilities offered, particularly Docker. This e-book has provided a complete look into that transition, beginning with the preliminary phases of grasping Docker's architecture and progressing to a deep dive into integrations with other cutting-edge software marvels such as Kubernetes.

At the beginning of the e-book, we began by delving into the fundamentals of Docker. More specifically, we uncovered its architecture and the primary components responsible for its operation: images, containers, and the Docker Daemon. These fundamental components give Docker its extraordinary strength while also making it a very user-friendly platform. Docker's ability to encapsulate applications and their dependencies into consistent environments (containers) has revolutionized software development, testing, and deployment. Containers provide an entirely new level of portability, scalability, and productivity to the table.

However, having a basic understanding of Docker's architecture is only the beginning of the journey. The readers of this e-book were taken on a hands-on trip that began with installing Docker, familiarizing themselves with fundamental commands, and gradually expanding their participation by generating Docker images, managing them, and examining the lifecycle of Docker containers. Docker's potential was revealed throughout the entirety of this process, along with how it makes typically challenging activities easier to accomplish.

The potential of Docker is not restricted to only the creation of isolated containers. As we progressed through the chapters, we became more familiar with Docker's rich networking and storage solutions. Due to these capabilities, applications running inside Docker containers can now communicate with one another, store data durably, and even distribute the workload over numerous instances. We took a deep dive into Docker Compose, an application that helps define and manage multi-container Docker applications and exemplifies Docker's objective of simplifying complicated processes.

Perhaps one of the most enlightening sections of this e-book was the exploration of Docker's integration with other tools and platforms, especially Kubernetes. Docker and Kubernetes, while often spoken about interchangeably, serve distinct but complementary roles. While Docker provides the framework and tools for containerizing applications, Kubernetes takes over the orchestration, ensuring these containerized applications run efficiently and reliably at scale. The synergy between these technologies paves the way for a new era of cloud-native applications.

But what truly sets Docker apart in the tech world is its dedication to security and efficiency. Through the chapters dedicated to these aspects, readers gained insight into Docker's provisions for running containers securely, ensuring data persistence, optimizing image builds, and monitoring and logging container activities. The importance of these aspects cannot be overstated in today's environment, where data breaches can have catastrophic consequences and where efficiency directly translates to cost savings and improved user experiences.

The future's potential became evident as we delved into the final chapters, discussing emerging technologies in the container space and Docker plugins and extensions. The software deployment and development world is evolving at an unprecedented pace, with Docker and container technology at its forefront. The integration of Docker with platforms like Kubernetes, the rise of plugins and extensions, and the constant innovation in the container space all point towards a future where applications are more resilient, scalable, and consistent than ever before.

In summing up our Docker journey through this e-book, one can't help but appreciate the transformative impact Docker has had on the software industry. It has redefined norms, set new standards, and paved the way for innovations previously considered far-fetched. Like any technology, continuous learning, exploration, and adaptation are the key to harnessing Docker's full potential.

While this e-book has provided a comprehensive overview and deep dive into Docker's world, it's essential to remember that the tech landscape is ever-evolving. As Docker continues to grow and innovate, there will undoubtedly be more to learn, explore, and implement. The knowledge acquired from this e-book is a solid foundation, but the journey with Docker, as with any transformative technology, is ongoing. Embracing the changes, staying updated with the latest trends, and constantly integrating new learnings into practice will ensure that professionals and organizations remain at the cutting edge of software deployment and development. As showcased in this e-book, the Docker journey is not just a technical evolution; it's a testament to human ingenuity, persistence, and the relentless pursuit of innovation.

Emphasizing the importance of continuous learning in the tech space

In an age where technological advancements dominate the landscape, adapting to rapid changes becomes a necessity rather than a luxury. The tech space is distinct in its pace, dynamism, and transformative capabilities among the various sectors that influence our daily lives. In such an environment, there's one undeniable truth — continuous learning is not just a recommendation; it's an imperative. The very nature of the tech industry, its benefits, challenges, and the opportunities it offers, underscores the critical importance of a commitment to never-ending education.

Historically, the world witnessed technological revolutions spaced out over decades, if not centuries. In contrast, the modern era sees groundbreaking technological shifts nearly every year. From the rise of the internet to the prevalence of smartphones and the emergence of artificial intelligence, quantum computing, and blockchain, there is a relentless barrage of innovation. Such fast-paced changes mean that skills and knowledge that were relevant even a few years ago might now be obsolete. Continuous learning, therefore, is the only pathway to stay relevant, informed, and competent in such a fluid ecosystem.

The tech industry is marked by its fierce competitiveness. Companies are in a perennial race to out-innovate their competitors. For professionals in this space, this translates to constantly upgrading their skills. In extreme cases, stagnation can mean missed job opportunities, career plateaus, or even obsolescence. Continuous learning isn't just about personal development; it's also about survival in an aggressive marketplace. When professionals commit to learning, they're not just enhancing their resumes but ensuring their relevance in an industry that doesn't wait for laggards.

The tech space isn't evolving just for the sake of change. Each advancement promises to solve problems, improve efficiencies, and enhance the quality of life. However, harnessing these benefits isn't straightforward. It requires understanding the technology at hand profoundly and its implications. For instance, the rise of big data technologies promised unparalleled insights into customer behaviors. Yet, these vast datasets would remain untapped without professionals skilled in data analytics as well as machine learning. Therefore, continuous learning isn't just about keeping up with changes; it's also about unlocking the latent potential of these technological shifts.

Technological changes don't exist in a vacuum. They interact with society, influencing and being influenced by it. The emergence of deepfake technology, concerns over AI-driven surveillance, and debates around data privacy are just a few examples. For those in the tech space, understanding these ethical and societal dimensions is as crucial as mastering the technical aspects. Continuous learning, in this context, broadens one's horizons, ensuring that professionals don't just create technology, but also understand its broader implications and responsibilities.

Beyond the pragmatic reasons, continuous learning fosters a growth mindset, a psychological perspective coined by Dr. Carol Dweck. In the face of challenges and setbacks, individuals with a growth mindset view them as an opportunities to learn and improve. In the volatile tech industry, where failures are as frequent, if not more so, as successes, possessing a growth mindset can be a significant asset. It promotes resilience, adaptability, and a forward-looking perspective, traits invaluable in any professional.

While the importance of continuous learning in the tech space is evident, it's worth noting that the modern era also offers unprecedented resources to facilitate this learning. Online platforms, digital courses, webinars, and forums provide many opportunities for professionals to expand their knowledge base at their own pace and convenience. Therefore, the digital age's challenges come with the tools to combat them, making the commitment to continuous learning both a necessity and a facilitated endeavor.

In conclusion, the tech space's dynamism is its strength and challenge. It's an industry that promises unparalleled innovation yet demands an unwavering commitment to adaptability and growth. Continuous learning emerges not just as a strategy for personal and professional development, but as a cornerstone for navigating the tumultuous waters of technological change. Embracing this ethos of perpetual education ensures that professionals don't just survive in the tech industry, but they thrive, innovate, and lead. In the end, the commitment to continuous learning is a testament to the recognition that in the ever-evolving realm of technology, the education journey never truly ends. It transforms, adapts, and paves the way for a brighter, more informed future.

Final thoughts about Docker and Containerization

In the ever-evolving software development and deployment landscape, Docker and containerization have emerged as transformative technologies. Docker, an open-source platform, has revolutionized how applications are packaged, distributed, and run across various environments. As we reflect on Docker and containerization's journey, it becomes evident that they have fundamentally altered the software development and deployment paradigms. In this section, we will explore the significance of Docker and containerization, their key benefits, their impact on the IT industry, and the future outlook for these technologies.

Containerization, as a concept, is not entirely new. It draws inspiration from earlier practices like chroot, but Docker took it to the next level. Docker introduced the idea of creating lightweight, isolated, and portable containers that encapsulate an application and its dependencies. This innovation began a new era in software development, where consistency and reproducibility became paramount. Developers could now package their applications and all necessary components, ensuring that they run reliably and consistently on any system that supports Docker, regardless of the underlying infrastructure.

One of the most significant advantages of Docker and containerization is their ability to simplify application deployment. Traditionally, deploying an application in different environments was a complex and error-prone process, often plagued by "it works on my machine" issues. Docker eliminates this problem by creating a consistent development, testing, and production environment. Developers can package their applications into the containers, which include everything needed to run the software successfully. This container can then be moved seamlessly from a developer's laptop to a testing server and finally to production, ensuring the application behaves the same way everywhere.

Furthermore, Docker and containerization promote efficient resource utilization. Unlike traditional virtualization, containers share the host operating system's kernel, which makes them lightweight and fast to start. This efficiency translates to cost savings, allowing organizations to run more containers on the same hardware as traditional virtual machines. It also enables auto-scaling, where additional containers can be spun up dynamically to handle increased workloads, ensuring optimal resource utilization and performance.

Security is a critical concern in software deployment, and Docker has also made strides in this area. Containers provide isolation, meaning each container operates in its isolated environment. While this isolation is not foolproof, it adds a further layer of security by limiting the potential attack surface. Additionally, Docker provides features like image signing and scanning, which help ensure the integrity and security of containerized applications. These security measures have made containerization a viable option for organizations with stringent security requirements.

Docker and containerization have also had a profound impact on the DevOps movement. DevOps is about breaking down the silos between development and operations teams to allow faster and more reliable software delivery. Containers fit perfectly into this paradigm by providing a common language and environment for development and operations. Developers can define the application's environment in a Dockerfile, while operations teams can use tools like Kubernetes to manage the orchestration and scaling of containers in production. This convergence of development and operations has accelerated the software development lifecycle and improved team collaboration.

Docker gained popularity and spawned a rich ecosystem of tools and services. Docker Hub, for instance, is a cloud-based registry that hosts thousands of pre-built Docker images, making it easy for developers to find and share containerized applications and services. The availability of these ready-to-use images significantly reduces the time and effort required to set up and configure application stacks. Additionally, orchestration platforms like Kubernetes, Docker Swarm, and Amazon ECS have emerged to simplify the management of containerized applications at scale.

However, it's worth noting that Docker and containerization are not without challenges. One of the primary concerns is the complexity of managing containerized applications, especially in large-scale, production environments. Orchestrating containers, monitoring their health, and ensuring high availability can be daunting tasks. This complexity has led to the rise of container orchestration platforms, which, while powerful, require a learning curve of their own.

Another challenge is the ephemeral nature of containers. Containers are designed to be disposable, which means they can be started, stopped, and destroyed quickly. While this flexibility is an advantage, it can also pose challenges regarding data persistence. Storing and managing stateful data in containers requires careful consideration and additional tooling.

Looking ahead, the future of Docker and containerization appears promising. These technologies continue to evolve and adapt to the changing needs of the IT industry. New features as well as improvements are continually being introduced to address existing challenges and make containerization more accessible and efficient.

Moreover, Docker has become a de facto standard for containerization, but alternatives like containerd and Podman have gained traction. This diversity in container runtimes fosters healthy competition and ensures that containerization remains an open and evolving ecosystem.

Additionally, the rise of microservices architecture has further cemented the role of containers in modern software development. Microservices involve breaking down applications into smaller, independent services that can be developed, deployed, and also scaled independently. Containers provide a natural fit for microservices, as each service can be packaged as a container, enabling greater agility and scalability.

In conclusion, Docker and containerization have revolutionized the software development and deployment world. They have simplified application packaging and distribution, improved resource utilization, enhanced security, and fostered collaboration between development and operations teams. While challenges exist, the overall impact of Docker and containerization on the IT industry has been overwhelmingly positive.

As we look to the future, it's clear that containerization is here to stay. The continued evolution of these technologies and the growing adoption of microservices ensure that containers will remain a vital part of modern software development. Developers and organizations embracing containerization benefit from increased agility, scalability, and efficiency in the ever-evolving software development landscape.

In a world where technology constantly changes, Docker and containerization have left an indelible mark, reshaping how we build, deploy, and manage software. Their legacy will continue to transform the future of software development for years to come.

www.ingramcontent.com/pod-product-compliance
Lightning Source LLC
Chambersburg PA
CBHW052033150726
48002CB00002B/577